CHANGE READY!

How to Transform Change Resistance to Change Readiness

A Manager's Guide to Managing and Sustaining Change in the 21st Century Workplace

RITA BURGETT-MARTELL

Copyright © 2011 Rita Burgett Martell
All rights reserved
ISBN-13: 9781467978330
ISBN-10: 1467978337

ACKNOWLEDGEMENTS

This book is dedicated to my amazing clients who have shown their trust in me by seeking - and sometimes following - my advice. Over the past twenty-plus years of consulting, you've taught me that the greatest value a consultant can provide is to listen and never under estimate the ability of an organization or individual to embrace change.

TABLE OF CONTENTS

Introduction: Change is the "New Normal"   vii
"When will we get back to normal?"

Chapter 1: Create a Shared Vision   1
"What does the future look like and will it include me?"

Chapter 2: Understand the Impact   25
"How much will I need to change?"

Chapter 3: Refocus Resistance: Turn Resistors into Advocates   51
"I need to feel in control."

Chapter 4: Engage Stakeholders Effectively   75
"I need to feel needed to feel secure."

Chapter 5: Prepare People to Succeed   111
"Will I learn what I need to know to be successful?"

Chapter 6: Evaluate Readiness for Launch   137
"Are we really going to do this?"

Chapter 7: Sustain the Change   161
"I can't believe we ever did it any other way."

Chapter 8: Become a Change Ready Leader   181
"This is a leader I want to follow."

INTRODUCTION
CHANGE READINESS IS THE NEW CHANGE MANAGEMENT

"When will we get back to normal?"

Since Alvin Toffler coined the phrase "Future Shock" in 1970 to describe his view of the world as one of "too much change in too short a period of time," our society has experienced profound change in the way we work and how we live our day-to-day lives. So much change, in fact, that multiple books have been written, and an entire profession of change management consultants have emerged, to help us "manage" and/or "cope" with the magnitude of change.

I think most of us who remember the 1970s would look back on what Toffler saw as a time of "too much change" and see it as a time of stability - compared with the uncertainty we all live with in today's world.

Back in 1970 we could count on having a job as long as we did a good job. Loyalty pretty much guaranteed our employment security.

We didn't have to worry as much about another company coming in and taking over our company and deeming us "redundant."

We could learn a trade or choose a profession that we believed would provide an income to support ourselves and our family until we retired.

We could buy a home that we actually stayed in long enough to pay for, and build equity that would take care of us in our golden years.

Organizations could confidently plan for the future and develop strategic plans that spanned ten or twenty years.

So here we are today, 40+ years later, still attempting to cope in our current world of "too much change in too short a period of time."

What has changed since the 1970's is that stability and loyalty are artifacts of a bygone era. No longer can you count on having job as long as you do a good job. Professions or trades that we once believed would be around forever are no longer needed or have been replaced by technology. To remain relevant in today's world you have to reinvent yourself at least every five years.

Your job security today is contingent on you having the skills the current workplace requires. You – not your employer – are your true source of security. To succeed in today's world, you not only have to do something well, you have to be flexible enough to quickly master the ability to do it differently.

Corporations that were once seen as the source of our security, because they appeared to be stable and would be around for our children and grandchildren to work for, are short-lived due to mergers and acquisitions. This leads to a revolving door of CEOs and senior leadership teams that creates an environment where no one actually knows who they work for anymore.

The requirements for corporate growth and individual success are constantly being redefined by transient leadership.

Even if you're fortunate enough to keep your job, you have to adapt to a new culture where you might not be a "fit," and to new leadership expectations that you may not be able to meet.

Long range strategic plans are a thing of the past as businesses are required to focus short term on what they have to do today to be in business tomorrow.

An investment in home ownership today is as risky as investing in the stock market.

Alvin Toffler's prediction of "future shock" has become our "new normal."

Change is the "New Normal"

Many of us are still in denial about the meaning of the most recent economic crisis of the first decade of the 21st Century. We keep asking ourselves "when will it end? When will we get back to normal?"

And, the answer is: we won't.

Some of us are slowly beginning to realize that there is no "normal." There is only a never ending cycle of change, and resistance to it or acceptance of it, and then more change.

No sooner have we "adapted" to a new way of functioning then a newer way comes along to replace the previous "new" way that is now the "old" way.

And, quite honestly, it doesn't matter if we resist or accept change, it will still happen. Resistance and denial only guarantee that we will be left behind while others benefit from the opportunities change creates.

If we are to move forward with our life and not get stuck waiting for things to get back to "normal," we have to accept the fact that **continual change is the new normal.**

We can invest our energy in "coping" with the day-to-day reality of too much change in too short a period of time, or we can learn to be "change ready" and prepared to take advantage of the opportunities change creates. Change is not only an ending to the way things are, it is a beginning that may actually lead to things being better.

Surviving But Not Thriving

"Coping" makes us feel and sound weak. We may be surviving change, but we're not thriving.

"Change Ready" makes us feel and sound confident. We have the flexibility and capability to not only survive change, but to thrive as well.

This is true of organizations as well as individuals.

Over the past few years, industry-leading global organizations have experienced a geometrically-increasing rate of business change designed to improve market share, competitive advantage, operational efficiency, and shareholder return. Many senior leaders are reacting to the new normal of constant change by attempting multiple complex and large-scale change initiatives with fewer resources than ever before.

Change Readiness is the New Change Management

Although many organizations are quite competent at getting these business changes launched - meaning they are up and running - they fail to sustain the benefits the changes were expected to produce. This is due in large part to the fact that the behavior change required to sustain the change isn't identified, addressed or reinforced.

The change is managed well enough for a project to be considered "done," but not well enough for the benefits to be sustained.

Once launched, people attempt to revert to the "old way" because they haven't been adequately prepared to sustain the "new way."

Rather than producing success, multiple change initiatives are producing an unparalleled level of organization stress and uncertainty. Although there is a high degree of activity focused around implementing multiple strategic business changes, often simultaneously without any recognition of the cumulative impact to employees, or without "connecting the dots" to link the initiatives and explain how the organization and its employees will benefit from all this change, the success rate is actually disappointing. A recent study by IBM shows the sub-optimized or **failure** rates for all types of strategic change is at 70% or higher.[1]

Why is our current approach to managing change only working with 30% of change initiatives?

Is it because we really haven't learned anything in the past 40 years about how to effectively manage change?

Or is it that our old approach to managing change won't work in today's world. It's time to adopt a new way.

It's time to *change* how we approach change.

Change Readiness: A New Approach to "Managing" Change

I was at the forefront of the change management profession. I began providing change management consulting services to individuals and organizations in the early 80's, long before it was ever recognized as a profession.

I have worked with the change management methodologies every top tier and boutique consulting groups and technology firms profess to be the change solution that works.

What I've concluded is that they're all basically the same.

---

[1] IBM Study "Making Change Work" Copyright IBM Corporation October, 2008

The only difference I've observed between the methodologies is their terminology and level of detail. The names used for the phases, activities and templates are different. Some use more slides with pretty pictures, complicated models and impressive graphs. Others are more detailed and attempt to address the people issues by having multiple detailed plans and templates that do nothing to effectively engage and prepare people for the change coming their way.

I began referring to this approach as having a "plan for the plan for the plan" that must fit into the master plan and timeline, whether or not it makes sense from a "people" perspective.

The pre-defined "fill-in-the-blank" templates support a "cookie-cutter" approach to change where the client's problem must fit into the deliverables defined in the Statement of Work that consultants must produce to be paid, and may have nothing to do with what the client actually needs to successfully execute and sustain change.

What is similar among the methodologies is that they all have a tendency to be very structured and lack the flexibility to allow for cultural differences inside an organization or from one client to the next.

Too many change management methodologies have replaced the "people" aspect of change with an activity-based approach to managing change that overlooks the fact that the human reactions to change don't fit into a project timeline and template-based deliverables.

Change, after all, is experienced individually and the bottom line is that people – not project plans - produce outcomes.

The current way of managing change is based on project-specific change. The project has a beginning and an end. There are defined phases with defined deliverables and metrics that are indications that you were on track – or at least on track to meet the project timeline and stay within the project budget.

Change activities fit into project management plans with a defined beginning and end for a particular project. Little – if any – thought is given to how people may be affected by other changes that are occurring at the same time and the ripple effect that can have on multiple initiatives.

But, in today's world, change is continuous. There is no end.

In today's world, there is no such thing as a "small change." Change has a ripple effect that leads to other changes. Change in one area affects other areas. Change, much like a wild fire, can't be confined to one particular area or one specific group in today's inter-connected global workplace.

Could it be that the structured and well defined methodologies we've used to manage change won't work in our "new normal" world of continual change?

At the same time the world is crying out for innovation, the change management profession is still following their "old" methodologies.

> *We have to change the way we approach change to enable people and organizations to be "change ready" and not only survive, but also thrive in the new normal of continual change.*

Change Readiness is the New Change Management

The speed with which an organization can change and how quickly an organization assimilates change is a distinguishing competence in today's market place and can determine whether a company stays in business or falls by the wayside.

This doesn't, however, mean launching multiple change initiatives that affect the same people at the same time without understanding the impact and providing adequate resources required to achieve and sustain success.

It does mean equipping individuals – who will ultimately determine if a change initiative has a successful outcome - with the skills to be "change-ready".

The success of achieving and sustaining any major organizational change effort is dependent on the "readiness" level of the employees.

> *"Readiness" is defined as the degree to which employees are ready, willing and able to adopt and sustain change.*

If an organization has a critical mass of individuals with this change ready competency, it will be able to function as a change ready organization and survive and thrive in a world where the pace of change continues to accelerate.

The ability to effectively refocus change resistance to change readiness is paramount to accelerating change adoption. Merely providing employees with the skills to "cope" with change, doesn't move the organization or individual forward. It doesn't create a change ready organization.

Achieving complex change in an organization is most likely to occur when people are fully engaged in a cooperative process to creating it.

When employees feel confident about their future and connected to the organization's strategy and vision, they are less likely to resist and more likely to take an active role in making the change occur. Their change resistance has been replaced with change readiness.

What this Book is About

Although a lot has changed in the 40+ years since Toffler introduced the concept of "future shock," what hasn't changed is the fact that people still have the same fears, concerns and emotional reactions to change. We all have the same basic needs to feel safe and secure during times of uncertainty.

The new normal has redefined our source of security. Our security no longer comes from pledging our loyalty to large institutions. It comes from our individual ability to be "change ready" and prepared to benefit from the changes that come our way.

So, it would seem that an effective approach to preparing for change will focus on what the individual needs to do to become change ready, and what an organization can do to strengthen this capability in the way it engages employees and executes projects.

It's time to change our approach to how we attempt to accomplish change.

The purpose of this book is to provide a common sense approach that balances the **individual** needs required for change readiness, with the basic **organizational** requirements to achieve large-scale change, that have proven to be successful on the numerous global change initiatives I've managed over the past twenty-five years.

The approach described in this book is practical and not-theoretical. It consists of a repeatable and scalable common sense process that, if followed, will allow you to refocus resistance to building readiness for change.

It is based on my twenty plus years of learning what works and what doesn't work. I haven't quoted any "experts" in the book and have only used models and provided guidelines that I have found help clients identify and prepare for the impact of change.

The Goals of this Book

This book has three goals:

1. Provide you with the steps required to launch, execute and sustain change in your organization. Each chapter focuses on one of these steps.
2. Help you gain insight into what people affected by your project are thinking and needing – but probably aren't saying – that if addressed can turn resistance into readiness. This is indicated by the subtext in quotes under the title of every chapter. If you truly understand what people need to feel confident embracing change, you greatly increase your chances of sustaining change.
3. Develop your own change ready skills that increase your confidence in your ability to thrive during times of uncertainty and become a change ready leader that others want to follow.

    I've included a brief outline of each chapter and subtext below. The name of the chapter describes the step you need to take and goal you want to accomplish. The subtext describes the thoughts we have when undergoing change that must be addressed for the change to be successful.

CHANGE READY
How to Transform Change Resistance to Change Readiness
A Manager's Guide to Managing and Sustaining Change in the 21st Century Workplace

Chapter 1: Create a Shared Vision
"What does the future look like and will it include me?"

> This chapter describes the steps you can take to create a shared vision that is relevant for everyone effected, paints a picture of what the future looks like, establishes the case for change, and answers the concern employees have about their own future.

Chapter 2: Understand the Impact
"How much will I need to change?"

> The goal of this chapter is to provide you with a customizable tool that you can use to assess the real impact of change, understand that what one person sees as an opportunity, another will see as a loss, and have the information you need to honestly answer the question of how much change employees will be required to make for the benefits to be achieved and sustained.

Chapter 3: Refocus Resistance: Turn Resistors into Advocates
"I need to feel in control"

> Resistance is the typical reaction to change. In this chapter you will learn techniques for responding non-defensively to resistance and creating an environment where people can have their concerns addressed. You will know how to leverage the influence of resistors to turn them into advocates and understand how the need, we all have, to feel in control can be refocused to work for you.

Chapter 4: Engage Stakeholders Effectively
"I need to feel needed to feel secure"

> After reading this chapter, you will know how to go about developing a strategic engagement plan that ensures your key stakeholders are involved at the right time and in the most effective way to take ownership of the outcome. When we are informed and involved we feel like we're a part of what is happening instead of a victim of what is happening. When we believe our involvement is required for a successful outcome to be achieved, we feel more secure and less threatened by change.

Chapter 5: Prepare People to Succeed
"Will I learn what I need to know to be successful?"

> This chapter provides you with the tools to evaluate what people need to know, do and think in order for your change to be successful. You will also learn how to determine the most effective learning strategy to provide them with the knowledge they need, plus the reassurance that they will be prepared with the skills required to succeed, once the change becomes the day-to-day reality of how work is done.

Chapter 6: Evaluate Readiness for Launch
"Are we really going to do this?"

> What does it mean to be "ready" for change? In this chapter you will learn how to identify criteria for evaluating readiness for change at critical milestones throughout the project timeline, and what to do if you determine that you're not ready.

Chapter 7: Sustain the Change
"I can't believe we ever did it any other way."

> You will know that you have achieved lasting change when you hear people saying "I can't believe we did it any other way" instead of "this is not what I expected and I don't like it." The focus of this chapter is on what to put in place before go live to create the structure and culture that is required for the organization to sustain the change.

Chapter 8: Become a Change Ready Leader
"This is a leader I want to follow."

We can't have a change ready organization without change ready leaders. In the final chapter you will learn the requirements for becoming a change ready leader who is someone others want to follow. You will know how to make change readiness part of the DNA of your organization so that it becomes a core competency and is viewed as "just the way change happens around here."

How to Use this Book

Although I've used a technology-driven change project as a real life example of how the change readiness tools and techniques described in this book can be applied, they can work for any type of change initiative.

As you read my narrative about the people I will introduce to you and the ups and downs of their project, ask how similar this is to experiences you've had with projects you've led or participated in as a team member.

What actions – or reactions – of the people in the story can you relate to that may have contributed to the failure or success of your project?

After reading each chapter, think about what could have been done in a different way on your project to achieve a different outcome, or what you can do differently on your next project.

What changes do you need to make personally to shift your thinking from being change resistant to change ready?

As a leader, what behaviors do you need to adopt to be seen by others as a change ready leader who inspires trust and is the type of leader they want to follow?

At the end of each chapter you'll find a "A Manager's Quick Guide to Achieving Change Readiness" that provides a summary of the key action steps described in the chapter.

Following this you will see a section called "Change Readiness Thinking," that reinforces how we need to begin to think differently about change to replace a resistant mindset with a readiness mindset.

Use "A Manager's Quick Guide to Achieving Change Readiness" as a checklist to confirm that your project is on track or in danger of derailing.

Review the Change Readiness Thinking content to evaluate how your current thinking or attitude may be contributing to your own feelings of uncertainty or resistance you experience in engaging with others.

Surviving and Thriving in a World of Change

Change Readiness is a skill you can develop that will increase your capability to refocus on the opportunity change creates. Instead of resisting it – which won't make change go away anyway – you can learn to benefit from it. It's a much better investment of your energy and will increase your ability to survive and thrive in our new normal world of continuous change.

My hope is that this book will provide you with the awareness, knowledge and tools to become a change advocate, instead of a change resistor, and someone who is seen as a change ready leader that others want to follow.

Being "Change Ready" will give you the confidence to believe that no matter what change comes your way, YOU will be ok.

And in today's world where change is the "new normal," this is a skill that will benefit us all.

CHAPTER 1:
CREATE A SHARED VISION

"What does the future look like and will it include me?"

It was a cold and rainy day as I walked from the parking lot to the office of my new client. I had been hired to oversee the change management effort for a $40 Million project for a Fortune 500 client. Little did I realize that the below freezing temperature I was experiencing outside would actually be warmer than the temperature I would discover among the project's Executive Steering Team members inside the project team meeting room.

After two failed attempts, the company was trying once again to implement an enterprise-wide SAP System and achieve standardization of their global business processes.

The CIO attributed past failures to overlooking the organizational and people impact of the project, and had made a commitment that the change management activities required for success weren't overlooked in the next attempt.

I enjoyed working on global projects and was encouraged by the fact that Dennis, the CIO, understood that the leading cause of failure for technology projects had more to do with people and less to do with technology. Unfortunately, I would soon find out that this awareness didn't exist beyond the CIO level.

It quickly become apparent that the prevailing belief, among members of the project and leadership teams, was that change management

Create a Shared Vision

activities only provided a forum for people to complain and would slow the project down. The more prudent approach was to withhold information until the time came to go-live with the system and then just tell people what they needed to know to use the system or – better yet – let them figure it out on their own. This would minimize the time for whining and complaining about something they couldn't do anything about anyway.

It's amazing that in the world of constant change we live in, leaders often believe that the best way to implement change is to not let anyone know it is happening.

I met Cynthia, the project manager, the day before. She seemed nervous but excited to have been chosen to lead a global project with so much visibility throughout the organization. I left our first meeting hoping she had not been set up for failure by being asked to take on a project that had previously failed twice.

Cynthia's background was in technology and she really didn't understand what change management was all about. She did know that since the mandate had come down from her boss, the CIO, to pay attention to the "people" issues this time, she needed to make sure it was included in her project plan. She needed someone experienced to come in and just "do" change management so the CIO would stop asking her for her change management plan. She mentioned that the Global Steering Team would be meeting the next morning and invited me to attend if I thought it would be beneficial.

I knew that participating in this meeting would provide me with a good opportunity to observe Cynthia's leadership style, interact with the steering team members, assess the level of support that existed among management from the different regions and functional areas that would be affected by the project and possibly begin to identify why the project had been unsuccessful on the first two attempts.

It wouldn't take long for my questions to be answered.

Cynthia called the meeting to order and introduced me as the consultant who had come on board to "do" change management for the project. She was immediately interrupted when Charles, the director of the regional office in London said "Cynthia, my people want to know why we are spending the time and money to attempt this project for a third time. They just don't see the benefit. And, quite honestly, neither do I. We're one of the most successful companies in the world. It's obvious that we're functioning just fine without standardizing anything. We don't need this system and we certainly don't need someone to help us manage change we don't need to make in the first place."

I was anxious to hear Cynthia's answer to Charles's question. Unfortunately, she didn't have one. Her only reply was, "well Charles, as I'm sure you know, this project is one of our top ten corporate initiatives for this year."

From the groans and rolling of the eyes of the participants in the room, I could tell that this was the company line that had been repeated so often no one even heard it anymore.

It was also clear that they didn't have an answer to the question about the purpose and benefits of the project that people would listen to, understand and support.

The very people who were responsible for the success of the project couldn't explain why they were doing it. The question of "how will the business be better off in the future because we decided to implement an ERP system and standardize processes now," had not been answered for them by their leadership – who had since left the company.

I was willing to bet that none of them had been involved in the decision to buy the system, standardize the processes and launch the project in the first place. Although they were responsible for the outcome, they really had no ownership in the project.

Without a shared vision of the future, it was easier to focus in the present on their perception of unnecessary cost and inconvenience.

This was clearly a project in need of a vision.

Part of my responsibility is to ask the questions no one else thinks of, wants to ask or wants to answer. I decided to seize the opportunity that morning to do my job and, in the process, assess how responsive Cynthia and the leadership team would be to the recommendations I would make from that point on.

"Do you have a business case or vision statement for the project?" I innocently asked.

"Rita, I know this is your first day here," Cynthia responded, "but you just have to realize that we don't have the time to spend doing those things. We've already wasted a substantial amount of time and money on two failed attempts. We have to be successful this time or our future careers with this company could be at risk."

Stan, the Director of Marketing for the US responded. "I agree. We just need to get busy and do this." "Yea," Bill, the Director of Sales for the US

joked, "our only vision is to still be working here when this project is over." "And," Charles added, "I guess that would be the major benefit too!"
Well at least they have a good sense of humor I thought.

Why Bother With a Vision?

The scenario described above is repeated in project meeting rooms across the globe. It's amazing that managers who would never think of beginning a project without a detailed project plan, resource requirements and budget, will launch a multi-million/billion dollar project without clearly defining the project vision, gaining understanding among leadership and middle management on the benefits the company will realize, and building alignment on how the organization will be prepared for the changes required for the project to be successful.

There may have been a business case and a vision of an expected beneficial outcome when Cynthia's project was conceived. It just wasn't communicated down from the top level of leadership to the level of management responsible for its execution.

Organizations invest millions of dollars in new technology, make decisions to standardize processes, and/or restructure departments without taking the time to explain why or to paint a picture of a future that will motivate employees to embrace the changes they will be required to make in the present.

If all managers know is that the mandate from above is to "just do it," they aren't prepared to explain to their employees what will happen, how they will be affected and why this will be an improvement over the present. This creates an environment where people feel confused, ignored and have little investment in the outcome.

This is not a recipe for success.

People need to believe that the benefit of change will be worth the uneasiness they will experience during the transition from the present to the future. Otherwise, they only have reasons to resist instead of support to think about and act on.

Without a clear picture of the future,
it's difficult to gain support for change in the present.

I decided that my vision for the best outcome of the meeting that morning, was to gain agreement from the team to reserve time on the agenda the following week to at least brain storm what the possible benefits from the project could be. We needed to replace the reasons to resist with reasons to support that people could understand and champion. Otherwise, we wouldn't be able to build support for the changes the project would bring.

I knew there was a glimmer of hope when Jo Anne, the director from Cape Town said, "I think it might help us to remember that one of the lessons learned that the previous project team shared with us was the lack of a clear statement of the project's purpose or benefits. No one was able to clearly articulate what the project was all about and why we're doing it."

When Hans, the Director of European Operations from Germany agreed, I could see my vision of success for this meeting becoming a reality.

"Well," said Hans, "I've heard my friends in the US say that the definition of stupidity is doing the same thing and expecting different results. Maybe we should take a little different approach this time. We won't realize the benefits of lessons learned from previous projects if we don't apply them to our project, we'll simply repeat the mistakes of the past. Rita, how much time will it take to do this vision thing you're talking about?"

"I've worked with teams who were able to do this in 30 minutes and others who took two days," I replied.

"We want to hear about the 30 minute version," Stan responded.

"Why don't I send all of you a description of the process we can follow along with some information I will ask you to commit to getting back to me by the end of the week. If we can add 30 minutes to the agenda for next week's meeting, and you agree to follow the process I recommend, I believe we can do this rather quickly."

"We may need to devote 10 or 15 minutes at each meeting for the next 3 or 4 weeks to refine what we come up with," I continued, "but I believe that will be time well spent and will provide us with valuable information to build on at each phase of the project. If you think it's a waste of time after the first couple of attempts, then we can drop it."

Through my 20+ years of consulting I've learned that the best approach to gaining agreement on next steps is to provide people with one step that's easy to say yes to and a way to opt out after that if they find it doesn't work for them.

> *Successful change comes from building agreements along the way.*
> *Little steps can lead to big results.*
> *Small changes build the foundation for bigger changes.*

My immediate goal was to change the mindset and behavior of the people who would be responsible for the successful implementation of this project. I knew that if I could do that, the probability of a successful implementation enterprise-wide was greatly increased.

"That sounds reasonable to me," Hans replied. "Unless one of you can come up with a better approach, I say we do this."

When no one responded negatively, I knew I had just found, in Hans, my influencer on the team. Even though Hans didn't have the title of project manager, it was obvious that the team valued his opinion and would agree with his recommendations.

"Good," I responded, "I will plan on sending you the information I described by the close of business tomorrow.

The Value of a Shared Vision

A vision provides a bridge to link the present to the future. Creating a picture of the future in the minds of those affected by change is an important first step in the change planning process that is often overlooked. Helping people see that this is a future that can include them, and may even be better than what they have now, creates an opportunity to build readiness and lessen resistance right from the start.

Change pushes us out of our comfort zone and into an in-between state that is uncomfortable and scary. This is a transition we must go through for change to occur, but one that few of us will choose to embark on without a vision of an outcome that we think will be better than what we're leaving behind.

Employees look to leadership to paint a picture of what the future will look like, explain how it will benefit them, guide them through the journey to achieve it and hopefully reassure them that they won't be left behind.

It's difficult to get people to follow you if they don't know where you're leading them. Why wouldn't someone want to hang onto the present when all they have to replace it with is an undefined future with no clear benefits?

Can you imagine telling someone that you want to take them on a long, uncomfortable trip but you don't know where you're going, you don't know why and you don't have any idea of how you're going to get there or how they'll benefit by going along on this journey with you. But, "just trust me and everything will be ok."

They would probably come up with all kinds of reasons not to go.

We can use this same analogy to understand how resistance is triggered in an organization. When change is introduced without a vision that paints a picture of the destination and the benefits that will be realized when that destination is reached, the change is all that's real.

Just as you would never begin a trip without knowing your final destination, neither should you expect your employees to support a change initiative without a clear picture of what their future will look like once the change has been realized.

The "just-trust-me-I'll-take-care-or-you" approach doesn't work in today's uncertain world where trust isn't easily given.

You may not have all the answers. But, if you can't at least define the expected outcome, you aren't ready to do the project.

You could end up like the Children of Israel, wandering around in the dessert for 40 years looking for the Promised Land but not recognizing it when you find it.

I knew that first morning that it was a critical first step for me to work with the Executive Steering Team to create a shared vision of the future they would be willing to work together to achieve.

In addition to defining a benefit for the organization, they each had to see a benefit for their department and for them personally – other than keeping their job as Bill joked.

Linking a Shared Vision to a Shared Problem.

Someone once told me that you must first have agreement on the problem to have agreement on the solution. Over the years, I've learned that

Create a Shared Vision

this is true. If individuals believe the change you are proposing will solve their problem, there is less reason to resist.

Linking a shared vision to a specific problem that crosses the organization can dramatically affect how team members, regions and departments view the project as well as how they interact with each other. It creates an opportunity to bridge any gaps that exist across the silos since the focus shifts from arguing about who needs to change to working together to solve a common problem that requires change across the organization.

Focusing on a shared solution to a shared problem can make the purpose of the project more relevant to the individual than focusing on high-level benefits the organization will realize but the individual can't relate to.

The department manager is in the best position to interpret the organizational vision in a way that links it to solving a specific business problem people in his or her department can relate to. By doing this, they also become the "owner" of the change at the local level, which is where the successful or unsuccessful implementation of change is actually determined.

A project vision becomes a shared vision and is more powerful if it is defined on 3 levels:

1. Organization: What is the desired outcome for the company (we)
2. Department: What is the desired outcome for your department (us)
3. Individual: What is the desired outcome for the employee (me)?

Describing the desired future on these three levels helps everyone begin to understand how they fit into the bigger picture as well as the importance of their role in achieving a successful outcome. It goes a long way in building support by creating a feeling of continuing to be a part of something instead of a fear of possibly being left behind: *"Maybe the future will include me."*

Including others in the visioning process, makes it possible for them to share the desired vision with you. It's no longer something that is being done to them. It may actually turn out to be something that is better for them. Because you've involved them in the process, they now have a role in creating the future.

Resistance is diminished and readiness for change is increased when individuals have a clearer understand of what's going to be different, why this change needs to occur, how they will be involved and how this could be better for them. They can now become an "owner" of the future instead of a "victim" of the future.

We typically don't resist what we have a role in creating.

The process for developing a shared vision across the 3 levels of the organization is described in greater depth below.

Level 1: Link the Future of the Organization to the Future of the Individual

While the case for change may have been established on the executive level, this information may not have trickled down to – or been understood by - the people in your department.

Individual employees look first to their immediate manager to determine if the change is a move in the right direction, or one that will ultimately threaten their future. The vision that has been developed on the executive level will be interpreted through the lens of "what this means to me" on the local level.

1. The first question employees will want answered is "why is the company doing this?"
2. The second is "how will this make us more successful?"
3. The third is "how will I be affected?"

Of course what they are really asking is: "Will the future include me?"
They will be expecting you, as their leader, to have the answers.

Level 2: Link the Future of the Organization to the Future of the Department

While you may not have been involved in making the decision on the executive level that will require changes in your department, you do have the power to create an environment in your area that creates support or resistance for the change initiative. You can do this by clearly defining and communicating what the future will look like for your department once the change is realized. Your employees will want to know the answers to the following questions:

Create a Shared Vision

1. How does our department fit into the bigger picture?
2. Why does our department have to change?
3. What will be different?
4. What does success for our department look like?

Again, what they are really asking is: *"Will the future include me?"*

Level 3: Link the Future of the Department to the Future of the Individual

The final step in creating a shared vision is to link the vision to the individual employee level. You must make it real for them.

A vision statement that makes sense on the executive level may not be as compelling at the employee level. Again, your role as manager is to interpret the corporate vision for them in a way that helps them understand what this means to them in their day-to-day role. They will want to know:

1. What does "achieving competitive advantage" or "being best in class" or "increasing profitability" - or any other "corporate-jargon" that you've used in your vision statement - really means to the way I do my work on a day-to-day basis?
2. How will this change affect my future?
3. What do I have to know or do to be successful?
4. How will I be prepared?

Again, what they are really asking is: *"Will the future include me?"*

"Cascading" Change Readiness

The approach we've described above cascades ownership for change throughout the areas affected by change. We'll be reapplying the cascading approach in subsequent chapters throughout the book. In this chapter we've kicked off the cascading approach by applying it to the development of a shared vision.

The vision is defined on the executive level by the Executive Steering Team. Each member of the Executive Steering Team then duplicates the process with his or her direct reports who are responsible for repeating the process with their direct reports.

The vision gets "tweaked" along the way to tailor the benefits to each area or reinterpret them in words employees in different regions or departments can better understand. The core vision that was defined by the Executive Steering Team, however, should not change. What often happens in going through this process is that people begin to realize that their problems are more similar than they are different. What benefits one area will benefit other areas as well.

The cascading approach may appear to require more time. The opposite is true. Since real change takes place on the local level, this approach speeds up the readiness process by involving people in a meaningful way from the beginning.

Vision Plus

There are other components of an effective vision that, if agreed to in the beginning, will minimize conflict and confusion and make decision making much easier throughout the project. I call this "Vision Plus." The building blocks of Vision Plus are described below:

Vision

1. Creates a picture of the future that helps individuals understand the purpose and benefits of the project.
2. Provides direction and focus for the work required to achieve the vision
3. Aligns project activities and decisions to the vision statement.

Critical Success Factors

1. Helps define success for the project.
2. Provides guidelines for making decisions
3. Answers the question: *"We will know this project has been successful if the following exists............*

Decision Criteria

1. Defines the decisions that must be made for the Vision and Critical Success Factors to be achieved
2. Provides objective guidelines and justification for making decisions that lead to the realization of the Vision.
3. Helps define decision roles, including the individuals who own the decision, provide input before the decision is made or informed of the decision once it is made.
4. Answers the question *"How will making this decision lead to the accomplishment of the vision?"*

Measures – Metrics

1. Provides statistical proof that the project was successful.
2. Reinforces the validity of the expected benefits.
3. Metrics can be defined as changes in behavior, reduction of errors, increased customer satisfaction, reduced costs, increased profits, increased, productivity, etc.

Agreements among Stakeholders

1. Validates that the purpose and benefits of the project are understood and supported.
2. Confirms that the roles and process for making decisions defined above is agreed to and the people responsible for making decisions have been identified.
3. Answers the question in the stakeholder's mind of *"why are we doing this?"* and provides them with something to support rather than only the unknown or misunderstood to resist.

Vision Alignment

Organizational alignment with the project vision is required if the expected benefits of the project are to be realized and sustained. This is also a characteristic of a "change ready" organization.

Alignment is accomplished by linking the vision and critical success factors of the project to the department goals and the performance requirements of managers and employees. This won't happen without following the cascading approach to facilitate involvement in the Shared Vision process described previously.

Start Small and Build

I knew that presenting the Executive Steering Team with the Vision Plus approach initially could overwhelm them, increase their resistance and decrease my effectiveness. I sensed a better approach would be to start small with something they could agree to do. I started out by asking each of them to answer the following questions:

1. What benefits could we realize from this project, company-wide - and for my area - that would make this project worth doing?
2. What problem could this project solve for my area?

By tasking them individually with the assignment to come up with answers to these questions, we were really creating the vision for the entire organization.

Each member of the Executive Steering Team would be defining the benefits for the area they managed and that they would be responsible for supporting through the change process.

In other words, this would allow them to take ownership of the vision, and responsibility for implementing the change and realizing the benefits for each of their areas. Achieving this would put us in a better position to finalize the Shared Vision and develop the components of Vision Plus.

Crafting a Vision Statement

Any effort that requires more than one-page to describe its goal is doomed to failure. If the point of the program is complex, people lose focus -- and eventually lose their way.

A vision statement describes the future and communicates that the future will be an improvement over the present. It builds on strengths or overcomes weaknesses.

To reinforce what we've stated earlier, a vision statement should answer the following questions:

1. What problem will this project solve? (what will no longer exist)
2. What value could this project add? (how will it contribute to our/my success)
3. How will this contribute to the accomplishment of existing organization, department, and individual goals? (link)

Process for Creating a Vision Statement

To follow the Shared Vision approach, we facilitated a group discussion with the Executive Steering Team Members and coached them through the process of repeating this exercise with their departments. The step-by-step process we followed is described below:

1. Describe what the future will look like once the project is finished. (Vision)
   a. What will exist once the project is finished?
   b. What will be better?
   c. What are the existing problems that will be solved?
   d. What benefits will be realized?
   e. What will stakeholders see as beneficial?
2. Determine how success will be measured. (Critical Success Factors and Measures)
   a. How will you know the project has been successful?

b. What policies, procedures, actions processes, etc. that currently prevents the organization from realizing the vision or objectives of the project will end or be revised?
3. Identify the decisions that will be required to achieve the desired outcome described in items one and two above
   a. Roles
   b. Budget
   c. Process
   d. Etc.
4. Define the process for making these decisions? (Decision Criteria)
   a. Which will be group and which will be individual decisions
   b. Who will be responsible for making these decisions
   c. What is the timeline for making these decisions.
5. Validate understanding and agreement among team members on the Vision, Critical Success Factors, and process that will be used for making decisions

Future Pull Visioning

Another visioning technique that works well with some groups is to guide them through the process of working backward from success. This is a very creative process that may not work as well with a culture that needs to follow a logical structured process. It is a fun exercise and is very effective for groups who are "stuck" or really want to think out of the box.

The Future Pull process works backwards from an imagined future of unprecedented success to the reality of what must happen today to begin working toward making this future a reality.

The process is kicked off by asking participants to project themselves into the future where they are celebrating success. You can establish the timeframe based on how long the project is expected to last. They are asked to answer the following questions from the perspective of a future where this success has already been achieved:

Create a Shared Vision

1. What did we accomplish that resulted in such recognition and made each employee so proud to be a part of this project?
2. What obstacles did we overcome to achieve this level of success?
3. What actions did we take to overcome the obstacles and/or seize the opportunities that made this success possible?
4. What investment (time, money, resources, changes etc.) was required to take the actions to overcome the obstacles?
5. What will we do today (decisions, actions, etc.) that will put us on the path to overcoming obstacles and achieving this vision?

By executing this process first on an individual level, then small group, and finally full team level, buy in is achieved without creativity being limited.

The step-by-step process is described in more detail below:

Step 1: Describe Success: What did we accomplish?

It is the year _____. We are celebrating incredible, unprecedented success. We are fully enjoying this celebration of our success. Your task is to create a list of what we accomplished that warrants such a celebration.

Process:

1. *Participants are given 5 minutes to come up with their individual list.*
2. *Participants are randomly divided into smaller groups of approximately 3 to 5 participants and given 25 minutes for each member to share their list, eliminate duplicates, and agree on the group list that is documented on a flip chart and presented to the larger group.*
3. *Groups are given 5 to 10 minutes each to share their list with all participants. Duplicates are eliminated and similar ideas combined.*

4. *The flip chart pages are posted on the wall and the group is instructed to follow a "dot voting" process to identify the items they find the most exciting. Each individual is given 6 red dots. They are asked to place the red dots on the item(s) they find the most exciting. They can put all 6 red dots on one item or allocate them to the 2 or 3 they find most exciting. (10 - 15 minutes)*

Step 2: Barriers: How did we Overcome Obstacles and Seize Opportunities?

The results of the voting are announced. Each group is asked to identify the obstacles that were overcome and/or the opportunities seized to achieve each of the top 3 accomplishments that received the most votes from the previous exercise, while keeping in mind that this is the future where the obstacles have already been overcome and success achieved.

Process:

1. *Each group is given 20 minutes to come up with a list of obstacles that were overcome for each accomplishment and opportunities taken advantage of. In other words, based on the way we are today, (mindset, structure, roles, processes, skills, location, current expansion opportunities, etc.) what could prevent this success from being achieved?*
2. *What opportunities do we have today that, if we pass up and don't take advantage of, might prevent us from achieving this success?*
3. *Groups are given 5 to 10 minutes each to share their list with all participants. Duplicates are eliminated and similar ideas combined.*

Steps 3 & 4: Strategies: How did we do this?

As we continue to bask in the glory of our success and amazement at the obstacles we overcame, think about what actions were taken to overcome obstacles, seize opportunities and position us for success.

Create a Shared Vision

Process:

1. The groups are asked to come up with a list of actions, decisions, and/or changes required to overcome each obstacle previously listed. (30 minutes)
2. This information is shared with the larger group. (10 minutes each)
3. The group is then given 10 minutes to evaluate the actions they believe would be most beneficial to the growth of the organization (H = High; M = Medium; L = Low)
4. This information is shared with the larger group. Duplicates are eliminated and the highest benefit actions are listed on a separate flip chart.

Step 5: Strategic Direction: What can make the biggest difference and require the smallest investment?

The dot voting exercise is used to evaluate the level of investment (difficulty, change impact, resources, etc.) required for each of the high benefit actions identified in the previous exercise.

Process:

1. Participants are given green and yellow dots.
    a. A green dot indicates less difficult to implement.(Low change impact, less investment)
    b. A yellow dot indicates more difficult to implement but not impossible.
    c. Any actions considered impossible are left without dots.

This exercise takes the group from the future possibilities to the present reality and helps them formulate short-term and long-term goals.

The Link: Forming a Vision Statement

After completing Steps 1 – 5, we will have achieved the following:

1. Compiled a list of accomplishments that describe the future direction of the organization and form the basis for a Vision Statement
2. Identified the actions that are required to overcome obstacles that might prevent this future direction from being realized. This forms the basis for strategic direction and high-level implementation plan.
3. Prioritized actions that can be taken based on benefit, investment required and impact to the organization. This information is used to develop a high-level timeline for the project plan that is builds on quick wins, low impact, and greater utilization of resources that are all aligned with strategic direction and vision.

The Vision Statement creates the link from the future possibility to the present reality. It describes the future we aspire to that may appear to be currently out of our reach but not impossible to achieve if we are willing to make the investment required.

Process:

Using the information obtained from the previous activities, participants are asked to create the most compelling statement that describes the future. The group is asked to focus on the following:

1. What are the consistent themes that have been repeated throughout the day?
2. What is the common thread that runs through all the accomplishments talked about and obstacles identified? This may be based on customer, market, product, location, talent, skills, service, image, etc.

Create a Shared Vision

3. What is the mental image of the project that has been created from the discussions that have taken place?

Each group is asked to come up with 2 vision statements that capture the main themes that have emerged throughout the day. These are shared with the larger group and one is selected or an entirely new one is created that is based on similarities or new thoughts that are triggered as each vision statement is shared.

Next Steps: Owners & Actions:

The session ends with a recap of agreements and next steps:

1. What are the next steps and follow-up actions we agree to?
2. Who owns the agreed to next steps?
3. What is the deadline?

Following our cascading approach, the next step would be to share the outcome with each department affected by the project, solicit their input, discuss and finalize at the next Executive Steering Team meeting.

Actualizing the Vision

The Shared Vision, Vision Plus and Future Pull Visioning exercises can be challenging to work through but well worth the investment of time and energy.

Just don't make the mistake, like so many have, of working through this process, producing documents, checking it off on the list of things to do and then putting it on a shelf to collect dust.

The vision statement needs to be included in every communication and presentation made about the project. It must be something that can be repeated effortlessly by anyone in the organization who will be required to make some type of change to ensure its achievement.

It took a few meetings for the Executive Steering Team to agree on the purpose and benefits of the project they were responsible for implementing and to draft a vision statement they would share with their organization.

They weren't quite ready for the creative approach of Future Pull so we followed the more defined, logical, step-by-step Vision Plus model.

Although going through the process was frustrating for many, the exercise created a one team mentality with a shared vision and shared solution to a shared problem they could each clearly articulate to their departments and work together to achieve.

Working through the Shared Vision and Vision Plus Models as a team provided an opportunity for the Executive Steering Team Members to gain clarity, strengthen relationships, and speak with "one voice" about the project.

Following the cascading approach created visibility for each Executive Steering Team member. It created an opportunity for each one to begin to build support for the project in his or her area, establish a framework to move the organization from resistance to readiness and most importantly, to take "ownership" of the outcome.

And, Bill got to keep his job.

Create a Shared Vision

Manager's Guide to Achieving Change Readiness

1. Define and document a Shared Vision
   a. Describe the future
   b. What will exist that doesn't exist now?
   c. What problems will be solved?
   d. How will our day-to-day work world be better?
   e. What does success look like?
2. Be prepared to answer the following questions to make the Shared Vision relevant:
   a. Why are we doing this project?
   b. How will the organization benefit?
   c. How will my department benefit?
   d. How will I benefit?
   e. How will we know we are successful?

If you can't answer these questions, you aren't ready to launch your project.

3. Validate that the vision is a Shared Vision
   a. Shared Problem: Solves a shared problem
   b. Shared Solution: Developed by people affected by the outcome
   c. Shared Expectations: Agreed to definition and measures of success
   d. Shared Ownership: Achievement of desired outcome is owned by everyone affected
   e. Shared Sponsorship: Visible support for the solution across th organization

Change Readiness Thinking

Keep the following thoughts in mind to shift your thinking to a Change Readiness Mindset:

1. *Without a clear picture of the future, it's difficult to gain support for change in the present.*

2. *Why wouldn't someone want to hang onto the present when all they have to replace it is an undefined future with no clear benefits?*

3. *Why would anyone follow you if they don't know where you're leading them? Why would you expect anyone to trust you if you can't answer their questions about where you're headed?*

4. *You can't have agreement on the solution if you don't have agreement on the problem the proposed solution will solve.*

5. *Successful change comes from building agreements along the way. Little steps can lead to big results. Small changes build the foundation for bigger changes.*

6. *Involvement = Ownership = Success: We typically don't resist what we have a role in creating. The more people are involved in creating the future, the less likely they are to resist it.*

7. *Change redefines our vision of the future. The questions everyone wants answered during times of change are:*
   - *What does the future look like?*
   - *Does it include me?*

CHAPTER 2:
IMPACT: WHAT WILL BE DIFFERENT?

"How much will I need to change?"

Now that the Executive Steering Team shared a vision for the project and its benefits, it was time to look at the changes the organization would be required to make to achieve and sustain the benefits.

Agreeing on a vision is easy compared to the challenge of agreeing to make the changes required to achieve the vision.

It's fun to think about what could be. The possibilities are exciting. There's no limit to the imagination when anything is possible and you're only thinking about what you want.

When the realization hits that something in our world has to change to achieve our vision, we're less enthusiastic. Or, when we realize that somebody else has to agree to make changes for our vision to become a reality, we begin to realize that we alone don't control the outcome.

This is the point in a project where the rubber hits the road. When the actual "price" of the change is understood, the decision may be to put the brakes on and not move forward. Or, to move forward with the project and deny that the impact will really be that great and, even if it is, people will adjust.

If we put on our blinders to avoid looking at what the full impact of change will be, or move to a state of "denial" so we won't have to think

Impact: What will be Different?

about how much we'll need to change, people won't be prepared and the benefits of the project won't be realized.

Projects often fail because the true level of impact to the organization isn't identified and planned for. We often don't look at the ripple effects of change that reach throughout the organization, or what is required to not only be ready to implement the change but to sustain it as well.

A change ready organization is one that understands, accepts, and prepares for the reality that change doesn't happen without something or somebody changing.

Everything costs something. There is a cost of not changing as well that must be taken into consideration when we begin to consider not moving forward because the cost of change seems too great.

Not conducting an Impact Analysis early in the project increases the risk that the level of complexity - in particular the complexity of behavioral and cultural changes – will be underestimated in the early project planning stages. The environment required to support the cultural changes to sustain the change will not exist and benefits will not be realized.

Do *We* Really Have to Change?

We want something to be different. We want better results. We want things to go smoother. We want our work life to be easier. But, we don't want anything in our world to change to accomplish that. We're not the problem. It's the other guy - "they" – who needs to change.

"If only "they" would change," I often hear," this problem would be solved." Or, after all, it was "their" problem to begin with.

The reality is that the "they" we talk about includes us.

Whether or not we think we caused the problem, more than likely we're part of the solution. Changes will have to occur in our area for the organization to realize the full benefits.

> ***We wouldn't have a vision of something different
> if everything in our current world was ok.***

In today's global economy, there is no such thing as a "small" change. What happens in Des Moines affects what happens in Cape Town. Change in one area will lead to changes in other areas. The challenge is to think beyond our world and understand that what we do and how we do it, affects others and the changes they make changes our world as well.

But, at the point we begin to realize that the change required to achieve success means that we – or something in our world – have to change, support often turns into resistance. Suddenly, what initially seemed like a good idea no longer does.

This is exactly what happened on my project.

When I mentioned to Cynthia, the project manager, that our next big task was to do an Organizational Impact Analysis to identify the areas and job roles affected by our project and the type of change and level of change they would need to be prepared for, she responded with "do we *really* have to do that? Wouldn't that just scare people? Won't it create an opportunity for them to complain and come up with more reasons why we shouldn't do this and ultimately slow us down?"

She was partially correct.

Since Cynthia's definition of success for this project was to go-live on time and on budget with the new system, she had no incentive to spend time and money analyzing what the organizational impact would be or what would be required to address the "people" aspects of readiness. Once the system was up and running, she could go away and the business would have to deal with whatever happened after that.

The True Cost of Change

I've seen the "go-live and go-away" approach followed on many IT projects. It doesn't lead to the realization and sustainment of expected benefits or ROI. It only provides organizations with a system to use and gives IT a bad name.

When a company buys a software package or implements a new system, they have to decide if they are going to customize the software to support the way the business currently operates, or change the way the business operates to fit the technology.

It's easy to calculate the cost of customizing the software. The cost of changing the organization to fit the technology is more difficult to estimate and is typically not considered when the decision is made to purchase the software.

Since customizing software is expensive, leaders typically make the decision to implement "out of the box," believing this will save them money. They don't take into consideration the "people" cost of doing this that arises from the fact that business processes have to be redesigned to fit the software, and this will change the way people do their work.

All three elements, people, process and technology must be aligned to realize ROI.

People Control Outcomes

Technology projects are the greatest drivers of change in an organization, but the ones that are the least likely to recognize or prepare for the "people" impact from these changes.

This is probably why, according to a 2010 study by IBM, the success rate for organizations implementing change is lower than the failure rate. The IBM study reports the following outcomes:
41% – Fully met objectives
44% – Missed at least one objective
15% – Missed all objectives or aborted
In all, 59% of change initiatives failed to meet their objectives.

Barriers to Successful Change

Through their research study, IBM revealed these key barriers to successful change:
58% – Changing mindsets and attitudes
49% – Corporate culture
35% – Complexity is underestimated
33% – Shortage of resources
32% – Lack of commitment of higher management
20% – Lack of change know how
18% – Lack of transparency because of missing or wrong information
16% – Lack of motivation of involved employees
15% – Change of process
12% – Change of IT systems
8% – Technology barriers

Note that people factors account for the top three challenges and for four out of the top five. What often is considered the unimportant "soft and fuzzy" aspects turn out to be what makes or breaks change projects.

Ingredients for Successful Change

Getting the "soft" stuff right turns out to be more difficult than getting the traditional "hard" stuff, such as resources and technology, correctly aligned. These key ingredients for successful change, as revealed in the study, are:
    92% – Top management sponsorship
    72% – Employee involvement
    70% – Honest and timely communication
    65% – Corporate culture that motivates and promotes change
    55% – Change agents (pioneers of change)
    48% – Change supported by culture
    38% – Efficient training programs
    36% – Adjustment of performance measures
    33% – Efficient organization structure
    19% – Monetary and non-monetary incentives

The central learning from this IBM study is that people – not technology – control outcomes.

Unfortunately, organizations rarely look at the people aspects of technology projects.

The organizational impact – including the cost of preparing people for the change and the loss in productivity while people are adapting to the change – isn't included in the cost of the project. And, as the study proves, there is a high price tag attached to underestimating the "people" aspects of technology change. The overlooked "people" cost of an "out-of-the-box" decision, can be quite high.

I shared this information with Cynthia to emphasize the need to assess the level of people impact from our project and make the following key points:

1. Since people use the system, we won't be able to go-live with the system if people aren't ready to use it.

Impact: What will be Different?

2. People won't be ready if we don't identify what they need to be ready for.
   ➢ What will they need to know that they don't know now?
   ➢ What will they need to do in a different way?
   ➢ How will their thinking and behavior need to change?

In other words, how much will people need to change? What is the overall level of change the people of the organization will be require to make to realize the benefits of the project?

What is the true cost of the project when we take the cost of the "people" impact into consideration? And, what will the cost be if we don't?

Will the expected benefits outweigh the cost? If not, why would we do this project?

I convinced Cynthia that we needed to add an Organizational Impact Analysis to the project plan and discuss it at the next Executive Steering Team Meeting.

Successful projects require a full, realistic understanding of their impact, upcoming challenges and complexities, followed by specific actions to address them.

Back to the Future

The next meeting of the Executive Steering Team went pretty much as the first one had.

I explained the process and reviewed the tools and templates we would use to conduct the analysis and interpret the results. We had a brief discussion on the pros and cons of doing the assessment and I asked for feedback from each member of the team. Without their support and participation, we wouldn't be successful.

Bill was skeptical and agreed with Cynthia that this would just open up a can of worms and slow the project down.

Hans was supportive and responded with "how could we possibly proceed without understanding how our people will be affected and how they will need to be prepared to work in the new world. This is a requirement for success."

Regina, the VP of Canadian Operations – who had been silent in previous meetings, chimed in with "of course it makes sense. One of the reasons we failed with the past two attempts is that we never took the time to assess what the organizational impact would be or what it would take to prepare people to function successfully in the new world this project will create. I completely support taking this step and can't imagine why the rest of you wouldn't agree also."

Go Regina! Her response was unexpected but very welcomed on my part.

When Hans and Charles voiced their support, I found it interesting from a cultural perspective that the Americans were the ones who didn't support taking the time to do this.

Why does it seem that Americans are always in such a hurry to accomplish something that our motto has become to "just do it" without realizing that we'll only have to do it all over again because we probably didn't take the time to do it right in the first place. We could learn something from other cultures about the "best" way to approach people change.

So, with the approval of the Executive Steering Team, we moved forward with the process of conducting the Organizational Impact Analysis.

Change Impact: Real or Perceived

Let's define what we mean by "change impact."

First, change impacts people on an internal as well as on an external level. Some change impacts are real and visible to the outside world. Other impacts are perceived, based on how we interpret a situation, and visible only to us in our "inside" world.

Change is always interpreted through our individual lens of "what this means for me?" This lens is customized to reflect our own unique fears, insecurities, unrealistic expectations and good or bad experiences from past changes.

What you see as a small change, may be interpreted by someone else as a major change.

What you see as a change for the better, may be viewed by someone else as a change for the worse and one that will turn their world upside down.

Change requires a new way of thinking and behaving. At the extreme, change redefines our vision of our "imagined future." We thought we knew what the future looked. Once we hear that a change is coming down the pike, we're not so sure.

Impact: What will be Different?

We thought we were safe in the comfort zone of our secure day-to-day routine where we knew what to do and how to do it.

We were confident that if we continued doing what we had always done, we could keep our job. As long as you don't rock the boat, you won't risk flipping it over and drowning.

All of a sudden, another company buys our company and the future of our department is in question. Are we redundant? Will we still be needed?

How much will we need to change in order to once again, feel safe? Will we be able to make the change or will it be more than we can handle?

New technology is implemented that may eliminate the need for a human being to do the work we have been doing. Information that was once only available to us is now available to anyone at the touch of a button without including us. We feel less powerful, less important, and less needed.

A process is standardized and we have to learn a new way to do what we have been doing the same way for years. We may think the new way isn't as good as the one it's replacing. Our way really was the best way – or so we thought.

We may interpret this change as criticism of our way. Maybe it wasn't really that good. Maybe we aren't as competent as we thought we were. Maybe we won't be able to learn and function in the new way.

Will we be required to change more than we are capable of changing?

We can experience the internal impact of change from the moment we hear change is coming and before any change actually occurs in our external world. Whether real or perceived, change affects how we see our world and our place in it.

The "inside" as well as the "outside" impact of change has to be recognized and addressed if your project is to be successful. The effect of this perception on the success of your initiative cannot be underestimated.

Small Changes to Some are Big Changes to Others

The second point to keep in mind is that to be an effective implementer of change, you must understand that there is no such thing as a "small change."

Something is going to be different. Hopefully, this difference will be viewed as a change for the better, by you and your employees, rather than a change for the worse. Often, this isn't the case.

Managers may be in a position of implementing a change that really doesn't change anything about their day-to-day work but significantly changes the way their employees work.

Since nothing really changes for the manager or higher level leadership, they don't interpret the change in the same way or feel the same feelings of fear and loss the employee feels. Their lens is different.

That is why my first question for the Steering Team members in conducting the Organizational Impact Analysis was "so tell me, what's going to be different in your world after this change is implemented?"

The silence was deafening. After all, they were leading the change. They weren't experiencing the change. Because of this, they weren't as sensitive to how the change would affect the day-to-day working world of their employees or the impact uncertainty would have on employees' performance.

Change *Changes* Everything

The third point to remember is that change has a ripple effect that leads to other changes and may impact more people than we may have initially thought it would.

Making one change is like eating one potato chip. It's not likely to happen.

You can relate this to your personal life by thinking about a recent change you made in the way your home is decorated. You may have started out by thinking that the only change that was needed was a new coat of paint on the walls. Because of the ripple effect of change, you probably didn't stop there. Suddenly the curtains weren't the right color. The furniture didn't look right. The new paint in one room made the other rooms look bad.

That one change for the better made everything else look worse and led to more change until we think that, once again, everything "fits."

Impact: What will be Different?

The implementation of a new technology system or launch of a process design initiative will shine the spotlight on one problem area that someone decided needed improving, but will also highlight others that aren't working well.

Changes in a process will require changes in procedures, policies, SOPs, business rules, and possibly even changes in thinking and behavior to "fit" with the newly designed process.

Maybe we should restructure the department to support the new process. Maybe we really don't need two departments and they can be merged into one. Maybe it just makes more since to restructure the whole company.

The change that was thought to be only a small change that affected only one area has now expanded to include other areas and additional processes, affecting more job roles and increasing organizational impact.

The ripple effect of change produces greater impact to more people who will need to understand and be prepared for what will be different.

The point is that whether the change starts out as only a little process improvement change or as a larger change of restructuring the entire company, it's important to understand the full organizational impact may be greater than originally thought.

Employees may begin to question if the impact of the change will be more change than they can handle.

Cumulative Impact of Change

The fourth point is keep in mind is the cumulative impact of change.

It's a safe bet that your project is not the only one taking place in your organization. The organizational changes from your project may not be that great, but the cumulative impact from other projects, or other changes taking place in the company at the same time - plus the changes we all experience in our personal world - may add up to be one too many changes for employees. It's important to take this into consideration when conducting an Impact Analysis.

What else is happening in the organization that you may not think has anything to do with your project? But, since it affects the same people your project affects, it could also affect the outcome of yours.

The cumulative impact of multiple change initiatives can lead employees to question their ability to function in a world where it seems like everything is changing at the same time. They're being asked to change more than they can adequately be prepared to change.

Accurately assessing the overall impact from changes occurring in your organization increases your understanding of what needs to be done to prepare your employees for what will be different in their world. It makes it possible for you to honestly answer their question of "how much will I need to change?" and to reassure them that they will have the support they need to move through the transition.

Understanding impact prepares you to prepare them, thereby accelerating change readiness and greatly increasing the probability of achieving a successful outcome for all.

How to Conduct an Impact Analysis

An Organizational Impact Analysis basically answers the following questions:
1. What will be different?
2. Who will be affected?
3. Who can affect the outcome?
4. What is the level of change impact by area, role and company-wide

Although an Organizational Impact Analysis includes a Stakeholder Analysis, the scope of the Impact Analysis is much broader. The section below is designed to guide you through the process of conducting this analysis.

At the completion of the Impact Analysis, you should have an understanding of the scope of the change, be able to identify the level of impact on the organization, jobs and people, and determine what will be required to prepare employees to be successful once the change is implemented.

Impact: What will be Different?

Step 1: What will be Different?

I've provided an example of an Impact Analysis Assessment Tool that includes sample questions, that may trigger other questions that need to be asked, to assess the type and degree of change.

The categories represent the areas of an organization that may require changes so that people, process and technology are aligned and ROI can be realized. These areas could also be impacted by the ripple effect of change that wouldn't be recognized without conducting the Organizational Impact Analysis. The categories include:

Operations
Policies
Procedures
Job Role
Organization and Staffing

How to Use the Analysis:

1. Place an **"x"** by each category in the left column that you can answer yes to, and describes an impact, that will result from your change initiative.

2. Place a **"?"** by each category that you think may be impacted but will require more information to understand the full extent of the impact. If you think a category doesn't apply to you, leave it blank.

3. Evaluate the overall level of change (H=high; M=medium; L=low) based on your understanding of what will be different after your project is implemented and the degree of change from the way things are today.

The questions included in the example below aren't designed to be all-inclusive, but to merely provide you with a tool to begin analyzing the widespread impact of change. You will want to delete those that don't apply to your situation and add ones that are more suited to the change your organization is undertaking.

Impact Analysis Template

Category and Sample Analysis Questions	Impact H=High M=Medium L=Low
OPERATIONAL	**IMPACT**
Changes in work processes • Do you expect changes in the department's processes? • Are there questions you have about how work will be done that have not been addressed?	
Integration between groups and/or with other departments • Will the current flow of information between departments or within the department need to change or new communication roles be established to facilitate a new level of communication? • Do you need regular meetings between departments/groups? • Do you need to establish cross-functional teams or disband existing teams that will no longer be needed because of the implementation? • Do new teams or communication processes need to be established to ensure effectiveness? • Will your expectations of other departments change (timeliness of reporting, accuracy of reporting, etc.)? • Will you put any measurements in place to track dependencies and report their effectiveness or level of performance?	
External stakeholders • Will changes need to be communicated to customers, vendors or other external shareholders? • Will there be differences in the way you work with vendors or customers?	
Overall Operational Impact (High, Medium, Low)	
POLICIES and PROCEDURES	**IMPACT**
Policies and/or procedures • Will documents need to be changed? (SOPs, policies/procedures that need to be modified, clarified, or written)? • Are there policies or procedures that will be purged based on the new processes? • Will existing Policy/procedure manuals still be up-to-date?	

Impact: What will be Different?

JOB ROLE	IMPACT
Authorization levels or processes • Will the transactions that need authorization change (types, levels/people, dollar limits) • Will authorization levels change?	
OVERALL POLICY/PROCEDURE IMPACT (High, Medium, Low)	

JOB ROLE	IMPACT
Tasks performed • Will new tasks be required? • Will any existing tasks go away? • Will the complexity of the tasks change? • Will there be a change in the amount of time required to perform job tasks?	
Role/job impact • Will job characteristics will change? • Will combinations of tasks shift? • Do you expect major responsibility changes?	
Required skills vs. existing skills • Are the people in job roles currently appropriate for the way work will be done after the change? • Are you confident that existing employees will be able to learn new skills?	
New competencies required • Will people be expected to behave differently? • Will new knowledge be required that employees don't have today? • Will there be opportunities to bring new competencies into the department?	
Performance standards and/or expectations • Will people be expected to perform at a different level than they are currently? • Will performance evaluation metrics and rewards be defined to measure and reinforce performance expectations?	
OVERALL JOB/ROLE IMPACT (High, Medium, Low)	

Organizational & Staffing Impacts	IMPACT
Management Structure • Are there any reporting relationships that will need to be changed? • Will the existing management structure be modified to better fit with the new organization and sustain the benefits of the change?	

Assignments • Are there any issues that need to be addressed in the assignment of people within the new structure? • Are there succession planning needs that should be addressed in the new structure? • Will staffing levels change? • Will new job opportunities be created?	
OVERALL ORGANIZATIONAL & STAFFING IMPACTS (High, Medium, Low)	

Organizational Impact Summary

The template below can be reproduced on an Excel spreadsheet to document the amount of changes identified and then sort by level of impact. This provides you with a snapshot of:

1. The types of changes that will have the greatest impact on the organization
2. Changes that will require the most preparation
3. The departments or job roles that will be the most affected
4. Where the greatest change impact will occur

SUMMARY OF ORGANIZATIONAL IMPACTS

High Impact	Department and/or Job Role Affected

Impact: What will be Different?

Medium Impact	Department and/or Job Role Affected

Low Impact	Department and/or Job Role Affected

Risk/Reward Analysis: Must do; Have to do, Nice to do

The matrix below can help you evaluate the risk/reward effect of the changes you identified that have a high or medium impact on the organization. You want to ask the following questions:

1. Are all of the changes required for a successful launch?
2. Is it really necessary to make all of the high impact changes at the same time?
3. Can this be done in phases to lessen the impact?
4. Can there be a staggered rollout to different areas or job roles?

In other words, what will have the greatest benefit with the least impact?
What changes are "must haves" for a successful launch and can bring the greatest rewards to the organization? Which ones aren't critical and can be delayed to lessen the change impact?

RISK/REWARD MATRIX

Priority 1	Priority 3
✓ Most likely to require planning and action to be prepared for go live. Required or preferable before go live	✓ Most likely to require long-term organization design work
Priority 2	**Priority 4**
✓ Requires minor adjustments, that can be easily achieved and are preferable to have in place before go live	✓ Likely to evolve on its own in a reasonable amount of time and will not require a lot of preparation pre go live
Launch Depends on This	***Launch Can Happen Without This***

Working through the risk/reward analysis helps you focus your efforts on what you must have for a successful launch. This doesn't mean that the items listed in the Priority 3 and 4 categories aren't important. They may be beyond the scope of your project or "nice-to-have's" that can be addressed at a later date or by other teams.

Steps 2 & 3: Who Will be Affected or Can Affect the Outcome?

Once you've identified and agreed on the changes required for a successful launch and ROI for your project, the next step is to use this information to identify the impact by job role. An equally important step is to identify the individuals who have the power to affect the outcome.

Impact Analysis by Job Role

It's important to define objective criteria for rating a change as high, medium or low impact. As we've stated earlier, what appears to be a small change to one individual may feel like a big change to another.

The amount of training required to prepare someone for the change in job duties is often used as criteria. It would make sense that a large

Impact: What will be Different?

amount of time required for training would reflect a large amount of change.

There are other type of high impact changes however, such as change in leadership, location, department restructuring, culture changes, etc., that don't require training but still have a high impact on individuals.

The table below can be duplicated on an Excel spreadsheet to accommodate the size of your project. Additional columns can be added to evaluate the impact of the number of changes required by your project and additional rows for the number of job titles affected.

This tool provides a snapshot of the high impact job roles, based on the level of changes they are required to make, and the ones that are critical to a successful rollout of your initiative. This information allows you to tailor your efforts to address the needs of these critical stakeholders

JOB ROLE IMPACT SUMMARY TEMPLATE

WHO	TYPE OF CHANGE REQUIRED: Check each box with an "H," "M," or "L" to rate level of change as H=High; M=Medium or L=Low. Numbers can also be used: 3=H; 2=M and 1=Low								OVERALL IMPACT
Job Title	New Job Role	New Job Duties	New Procedures	New Process	New System	New Mindset	New Performance Metrics		Level of Change (based on total number checked)

Since the Job Role Impact links organizational changes to the individuals impacted, it is one key component of a Stakeholder Analysis.

There is a broader definition of "stakeholder," however, and a more in-depth Stakeholder Analysis that needs to be completed, as described in the section below, before the full impact can be accurately assessed.

Stakeholder Analysis

Stakeholders are defined as anyone in the organization who:

1. Will be "impacted" by the change
2. Can "impact" the outcome.

Critical Stakeholders are individuals who have a greater degree of influence or will experience a greater change impact from your initiative.

We've worked through the exercises above to identify areas of the organization and job roles that will be impacted by your project. Identifying those individuals who have the "power of influence" to affect the outcome of your project however, is just as critical to the success of your project.

Change Readiness can be accelerated by focusing your efforts on the needs of the critical stakeholders, both those "impacted" and those who can "impact."

Influencers: Power Where You Least Expect It

Stakeholders who can" impact" the outcome are typically referred to as "influencers." These are the individuals who can passively withhold support or are in a position to actively place roadblocks along your path to success. It's as important to create a strategy for working with influencers as it is to develop a plan to prepare those impacted by your project.

Influencers come in many shapes and sizes. They may have impressive titles, but just as often can come without titles.

It's easy to identify influencers based on their position in the organization. That's how they gain their power. Power comes from their title. They had something going for them in order to reach that level in the organization. This "something" may have been based on their knowledge and skills or simply on who they know. Either way, they have power that you can leverage to be successful.

The other "influencers," who don't have a title that would explain the power they have over others, aren't as obvious initially. They won't, how-

Impact: What will be Different?

ever, take long to emerge or be that difficult to identify. It's the individual who:

1. Everyone looks to for an explanation when something new is announced
2. Can redirect any conversation to what they want it to be
3. Chooses to ignore you – so everyone around him/her does as well
4. Has the power – either based on longevity or the willingness to confront – that instills a level of confidence in others that a leader may not be able to match.

Often, they are the people you would describe as the "trouble-makers" or the "thorn-in-your-side."

You must have these individuals on your side, even though they may be the ones you want to spend the least amount of time with or attempt to make an effort to get them to see things your way.

You may be insulted that they would even dare to question you or ignore what you say. But --- that willingness to question or ignore you --- is what gives them the very power you need to have work for you and not against you.

In the next two chapters, on Resistance and Engagement, we'll talk more about how to get the influencers on your side. The first step is to identify who they are. This knowledge makes it possible for you to involve them in a way that redirects their energy from resisting to supporting change, so that others will as well. "Influencers" hold a key role in determining the outcome.

The purpose of the template is to identify stakeholder groups and critical stakeholders within each group. It's also designed to provide you with space to gather additional information, such as their current level of understanding and support, priorities, expectations, roles and responsibilities that will be helpful in developing a strategy to gain their commitment.

Stakeholder Analysis Template

Area	Impact			Influence			Support			Expectations	Priorities	Challenges
Stakeholder	H	M	L	H	M	L	H	M	L			

As with the other templates, the Stakeholder Analysis Template can be reproduced on an Excel spreadsheet to accommodate the size of your project. You can have one for each department, region, functional area and/or overall enterprise for larger projects.

The Stakeholder Analysis is a living document that is updated at critical milestones throughout the project as you identify additional stakeholders and learn more about impact.

You will want to assess the current level of stakeholder support while realizing that this will change throughout the project. We will discuss more about how this happens and what you can do to maintain the level of support you need throughout the project in subsequent chapters.

Understanding the priorities and expectations of influencers will help you communicate effectively and honestly about what the project will accomplish.

Aligning the benefits with the priorities of the influencers, will greatly increase your chances of gaining their commitment. If you miscommunicate the real benefits or impact, you will only lose their trust.

The Stakeholder Analysis also serves as a roadmap for developing a Change Readiness Plan that is tailored to achieve the level of commitment required from the influencers to prepare for the level of organizational impact required to realize and sustain the benefits of your project.

The information from the analysis allows you to leverage the formal and informal power base in the organization to build the critical mass of support required to realize change and sustain the benefits long after the project ends.

Impact: What will be Different?

The goal is to obtain a high level of support from those with high influence in areas experiencing a high impact, and to avoid a low level of support from those with a high level of influence – especially in high impact areas.

However, don't assume that those with a low level of support in low impact areas can be ignored. An individual's influence can reach beyond his or her area and affect the thinking of their peers in other areas that may experience a greater impact and require greater support.

The ideal is to have a high level of support for your project from all areas of the organization.

Step 4: What is the level of change impact company-wide

The benefit of completing the various impact analysis described in this chapter is that you will have a more accurate assessment of the true organizational impact of your project and if the benefits will outweigh the cost.

You will know where the high impact areas are and whose support you will need for your project to be successful.

Once the true impact is understood, and the level of leadership support that will be required for the changes to be successfully implemented and sustained, an informed decision can be made about moving forward with the project. This is a critical decision point where you may find that the support you had for the project in the beginning, now turns to resistance once the full impact is understood.

Change sounds good as long as it's happening to someone else. When we find out how much we'll need to change, it may no longer sound like such a good idea.

Support Turns to Resistance

After the Steering Team completed their Organizational Impact and Stakeholder Analysis, a whole different view of the project and its benefits emerged.

Bill was thrilled, since his organization had to undergo little change and his position with the company seemed secure.

Hans, on the other hand, who had been my strongest supporter, became my most powerful resistor.

After he conducted the Organizational Impact Analysis for his area and began to realize that this change meant *real change* for his area, his response was "there is no way in _____ my region will do this."

"The impacts we'll experience and the amount of change we'll have to undergo - when balanced with the benefits we'll experience - just don't make sense for us. There is no way in good conscience I can support this," he adamantly stated.

Charles, from England, jumped in and said "I totally agree. There is no way Europe can support this. It's just too much change."

Of course, this was shocking for me and for the Steering Team. Would the team member's reaction be to take a deep breath and listen to what Hans and Charles were really saying, and try to understand and address their concerns?

Or, would we say "too bad for you. You were the biggest supporters of this project until you found out you have to change. Now we expect you to backup that verbal support with the leadership that will provide us with the momentum we need to be successful?"

In the next chapter on Resistance you'll find out.

A Manager's Quick Guide to Achieving Change Readiness

1. Define what will be different as a result of your project
   a. Compliance, policy, process and/or procedural changes
   b. Job role responsibilities and/or performance expectations
   c. Management or department structure
   d. Cultural values and behavior
2. Assess the change impact to understand how to prepare the organization
   a. What type of change?
   b. What level of impact?
   c. What are the potential "internal" impacts based on perceptions?
   d. What other changes are going on that could affect your project or touch the same people your project will impact?
   e. Will the benefits of change outweigh the cost of change?
3. Identify who will be impacted and who can impact the outcome
   a. Who will have to behave and/or think differently because of your project?
   b. Who has the power of influence – formal or informal - to block success?
   c. Who are the critical stakeholders that will experience the greatest change or have the most influence?
4. People control outcomes.
   a. Evaluate your project against the key ingredients of success identified in the IBM Study. Have you have overlooked any "people factors" that could prevent success?

Change Readiness Thinking

Keep the following thoughts in mind to shift your thinking to a Change Readiness Mindset:

1. A change ready organization is one that understands, accepts, and prepares for the reality that change doesn't happen without something or somebody changing.

2. We wouldn't have a vision of something different if everything in our current world was ok.

3. Change has a ripple effect. Change in one area will lead to changes in other areas.

4. There is no such thing as a small change. What seems insignificant to you may seem huge to others.

5. People are affected by their interpretation of the change. "Internal "impact can occur before anything actually changes externally.

6. If we put on our blinders to avoid looking at what the full impact of change will be, or move to a state of "denial" so we won't have to think about how we'll need to change, we won't be prepared and the benefits of the project won't be realized.

7. Understanding the impact of change to your employees prepares you to prepare them.

CHAPTER 3: REFOCUS RESISTANCE

"I need to feel in control."

"I knew it was a mistake to do that Impact Analysis," Cynthia responded with clear anger in her voice. "It only emphasized the bad things about this project and none of the benefits. Now we've lost Hans's support and his area is one of the most critical to the success of the project."

"Isn't it better to know what some of the issues are now Cynthia," I responded. The Impact Analysis provided valuable information that will help us better prepare for the implementation of the project. People who are resisting have reasons that make sense to them. We need to know what these reasons are so we can address them and not allow them to continue to grow."

"Resistance is our way of protecting ourselves from losing. What is Hans afraid of losing? Or, maybe a better question might be what is making Hans feel that he's lost control? If he's beginning to realize that his area will change in ways he didn't imagine, and he's feeling powerless to do anything about it, resisting gives him back his power and the feeling of being in control. We have to respond to him in a way that redirects his power back to supporting the project and preparing for the changes his area will be required to make to realize the benefits. He's not powerless. He's just feeling like he is at the moment."

Refocus Resistance

Cynthia's next response let me know that she hadn't heard what I said. She was resisting my thoughts on how to respond to resistance. To increase my effectiveness with Cynthia, I had to "refocus" what I was saying in a way that would address her fears instead of Hans's fears.

"It would be better if they didn't know about all the changes – or at least not now," she responded. "This will only slow us down. I need to make sure we go live with this system on schedule. The business is responsible for making sure their people are prepared. That's not my problem."

"So", I responded, "without the impact analysis, people – especially Hans- wouldn't have known what was coming, wouldn't have resisted, and wouldn't have been prepared?"

"That's right." she responded.

"But," I replied, "you would have gone live with a system no one would be prepared to use. How could you define that as success?"

"They would have figured it out," she said to my dismay.

"Well," I replied, " it seems doubtful to me that your leadership would have been happy about investing millions of dollars in a new system that people couldn't use because they hadn't been prepared to use it. And, they weren't prepared to use it because you didn't identify the changes they needed to be prepared to make. Not to mention, losing the potential ROI that could have been realized from making the process and organizational changes that would maximize the benefits from the technology. Do you think that might have reflected badly on you?" I asked.

"Yes, but shouldn't someone have thought through this before we decided on the technology," she asked?

"Yes," I replied, "when your company made the decision to purchase the system they also made the decision to implement the system as is. They thought it would be too expensive to customize the technology to fit your current processes and organizational structure and didn't consider the cost of the organizational changes that would be required to fit the technology."

"When they made that decision, they also made the decision to *change* the organization to fit the technology. This means change – big change – to the way people do their work, which leads to resistance – big resistance – from the people who have to make those changes. You're now dealing with the realization among the Steering Team members about the real impact of this project to their area, and they aren't happy about it. But, we have to remember that change readiness isn't about making people happy, it's about making sure that people affected by the change are prepared for the change."

"We have to be honest in our conversations with people who are going to be affected by this project. If it is going to be a rough ride we need to tell them that."

> **Being honest doesn't create more fear.**
> **It builds trust and a desire to support one another through the changes.**

"We have to create a safe environment for people to express their concerns and objections so that we can address them. When people feel they have been heard, even if they don't like what they hear, their level of trust increases, resistance decreases and they are more likely to accept the changes they are being asked to make."

"Hans felt safe expressing his concerns. That's good. It's better than having him agree and then sabotaging us later. We now know what to expect from his area and we can put a plan in place to respond to issues we know we'll have to address."

"We also need to keep in mind that while Hans felt comfortable expressing his concerns, other members of the Steering Committee didn't."

"Charles was the exception, but he has never been our strongest advocate so that was to be expected. He seized the opportunity Hans presented to restate his opposition to the project."

"I have a feeling that if we are able to regain Han's support, Charles will follow. I also have a feeling that the view they both expressed is shared by others on the team as well."

"So now what do we do?" a dejected Cynthia asked.

I could sense that she thought she would have been much better off if I had never shown up on the project.

People often think that organizational change consultants are alarmists who create more problems than they solve. The truth is, however, that while we don't create problems, we do shed a light on existing problems that no one wants to acknowledge - let alone address.

The resistance I was getting from Cynthia was not new to me. I've had many experiences where I have to respond to resistance from

Refocus Resistance

the very people I'm trying to teach how to respond to resistance from others.

Through my work with people at all levels of an organization and in countries all over the world, I've learned that human beings have common reactions to change:

1. We believe that change that affects us is only good when it's our idea.
2. We don't like it when people make changes that interfere with the way we believe our world should function.
3. We don't like it when people do things that puts us in a position where we feel powerless and see change as our only choice
4. We don't like it when people make changes that affect us without involving us in the decision.
5. We don't like it when people try to stop us from making changes we know need to be made.

As we discussed in the previous chapter, we don't often take into consideration the impact change has on others. We may be so excited about what we view as a new opportunity that we just assume others will be as well. What we don't realize is that:

> ***Our perception of gain may be someone else's perception of loss.***

Basically, we don't like it when we feel out of control. When someone is resisting our ideas, we feel like they are resisting us. We may think that they can stop us from doing what we need to do. We feel threatened and out of control, and try to regain control by attempting to suppress or ignore any resistance we encounter from others. Maybe if we ignore them, they will go away.

But, ignoring resistors doesn't make them go away. Often, it only makes them stronger. It provides people who feel powerless and out of control with something to hang onto to feel more powerful.

I had to realize that Cynthia was feeling like she was losing control of her project. I had to do what I could to help her regain that control. I had to apply my belief that resistance is a normal human response that tells us where we need to focus our energies to remove roadblocks that can prevent us from being successful. In short, I had to put into practice what I was preaching to Cynthia in order for me to be successful in overcoming her resistance.

> ***Resistance tells us where to focus our energies.***
> ***Ignoring it doesn't make it go away. It only makes it stronger***

"We recognize that resistance exists", I replied to Cynthia, "try to understand why it's there and focus our energies on how we can respond to it in a way that lessens the resistance and increases support."

"Now that the Impact Analysis has provided us with the information about what will be different, we can begin to work on what needs to be done to involve people so they will feel more in control of what is happening to them and better prepared for what will be different. This will increase their sense of security, lessen their fear of change, give them a reason to listen to what we are saying and eventually strengthen their support for the project."

"Remember, people are more willing to embrace change when they feel like their concerns are being heard and will accept 'bad news' if they feel like they've been treated with respect. Ignoring them only makes them feel more powerless and that resisting is all they have left to do to feel some sense of control over their day-today world."

"I don't have a clue about how to do that" Cynthia responded.

"That's OK," I replied. "I do. We can do this," I added confidently, because I knew that we could. I also believed saying this would lessen Cynthia's fears, refocus her thinking on what we could do, help her feel more in control of the outcome of her project and reduce her resistance.

I could tell she was beginning to see some benefit from having me around.

"There are basic principles of responding to resistance we can follow that will allow us to manage it because it will never go completely away," I began.

I restated the following points to Cynthia to reinforce what I had said earlier, since I wasn't sure she had really heard me the first time I said them.

1. **We need to simply recognize that in any group there will always be about 20% who aren't on board and that's OK.**

   This group will be made up of "detractors" who can be quite vocal and make this group seem larger and more powerful than it actually is. Hans is the most visible at the moment, but there will be more who have the same reactions he's having."

2. **Although there will always be whiners and complainers, I continued. 20% of people generally get on board right away.**

   They see the opportunities change creates or they just like the excitement of something new.

3. **60% will be open to it but want more convincing.**

   Concentrating your effort on the 60% who are bystanders – and their peers who can move them to the "on board" group - will reap the biggest rewards. It also provides them with the support they need to stick with their beliefs, which are more in alignment with yours.

4. **The people who are supporters, bystanders and detractors can also change throughout the project.**

   We have an example of that with Hans. You will find that with others also. Someone who starts out as our most vocal detractor can become our most vocal advocate later in the project. Out initial supporters can become "fence sitters" if they are influenced by someone in a position of authority who no longer supports the project. This is why we have to monitor our levels of stakeholder support throughout the project.

"Are you telling me that I'm going to have to continually convince people that this project is the right thing to do? How will I ever have time to actually do my job if all my time is spent responding to whiners," a frustrated Cynthia responded?

"Not necessarily," I replied. "The key to success is knowing who to respond to and who to ignore because their resistance really doesn't affect the outcome of your project."

> *You don't need a 100% agreement*
> *You do need a critical mass of support to be successful.*

"In the early stages of a change initiative we won't waste valuable energy on the detractors - unless they're someone who has the power to stop the project. Hans does. He's a critical stakeholder, someone who will be impacted by the project as well as someone who can impact the outcome of the project. We can't ignore him," I replied.

"Our best approach is to address his concerns and not to argue with or ignore his objections. No one wants to be told they're wrong or made to feel that their concerns aren't valid. Doing that will only put him on the defensive," I continued.

> *When you argue with someone's objections that becomes the focus.*
> *They won't listen to your solution because they're defending*
> *their objections.*

"We need to respond to his 'yes, but….' objections with a 'yes, and…' response. We need to listen to what he is saying, agree with him that **yes**, this will be a challenge **and** we will help him prepare for it and make it work."

"We also have to leverage the influence of his peers who do support the project and his leadership if necessary, to help us get him back on board."

"As we move through the different phases of the project, we'll see that people who continue to resist really start to stand out as more of their peers begin supporting the change. When this happens, we'll see the following:

1. The momentum we build will change their perspective, as they recognize the change isn't going away, and they'll decide to come along for the ride. This comes in waves and won't happen at the same time for everyone.
2. Their colleagues will start demanding a change in attitude from them as they begin to sound more like whiners and peo-

Refocus Resistance

ple tire of their negativity. Peer pressure will diminish their resistance. You won't have to do anything.

3. They will simply 'move on' elsewhere because they are no longer comfortable in this world. That isn't always a bad thing. The new environment that will exist after the change is implemented may require skills they don't have, or may be in conflict with their values and beliefs about how the workplace should function."

"Each of these possible outcomes are entirely valid and common responses to change as people move through the various stages of the Resistance Cycle. One of the most important steps in driving effective change is to focus on what 'is' working. It requires less effort from everyone involved and builds the positive momentum you need."

"As we've talked about," I re-emphasized, "there will always be some degree of resistance and who this comes from will change throughout the project."

"Hans started out as one of our strongest supporters and now he is one of our strongest resistors. He's a critical stakeholder so we'll need to regain his support, and I'm confident we will," I replied, hoping to sound more confident than I actually felt.

"After all," I continued, "there was something he liked about this project initially or he never would have supported it in the first place. He's not able to focus on that now because he's focusing more on the amount of change this will mean for his area - and he's probably thinking they can't handle it. We have to listen to what he is saying, try to understand where his resistance is coming from, and make every effort to get him back on board."

"I have a headache," Cynthia responded.
I didn't tell her, but I did too.

Twelve Basic Principles for Responding to Resistance

I asked Cynthia to read over the following Twelve Basic Principles for Responding to Resistance that summarized and reinforced what I hoped she would take away from our discussion.

I asked her to think about how the principles could be applied to her project and, more importantly, how she might modify her thinking and behavior to respond to others in a manner that will increase their support rather than reinforce their resistance.

I then scheduled a meeting two days later to work with her to develop a strategy for gaining back Han's support, and to design an approach she could follow to minimize resistance throughout the project.

Understanding and applying the Twelve Basic Principles, described below, will increase your effectiveness in minimizing any resistance you may encounter.

The Twelve Basic Principles for Responding to Resistance

1. **Resistance is a normal response to change that is sometimes hidden and sometimes overt.**

    It may be expressed verbally, but can also be expressed non-verbally through behavior. That is why you must pay as much attention to what people **do** as to what **they say.** Do their words match their actions? What people do is a more accurate reflection of what they believe.

2. **Resistance may be based on a lack of understanding of the goals, purpose and impact of the initiative and will diminish when people realize that the benefits of change outweigh the costs.**

    That's why clear, consistent and continual communication about the project's goals, impacts and benefits is so important. That's also why it's important to create a shared vision of the future that we discussed in Chapter One.

3. **Support can turn to resistance, however, when people understand the full impact of a change initiative and don't like it.**

    When this happens you are faced with the dilemma of deciding who to invest your energy responding to, and who you can ignore because they aren't a critical stakeholder.

    Answering the "so what?" question – "so what can this individual do that will prevent us from moving to the next phase or being successful overall?" can help you decide if your energy is better invested in getting them on board, or allowing them to move through the normal Cycle of Resistance to Acceptance described below.

4. **Realize that there is a Cycle of Resistance to Acceptance people move through from thinking "No Way!" to "I can't believe we ever did it any other way."**

   Resistance begins with a normal reaction of "you must be crazy, there's no-way I'm going to do this." If people don't get entrenched in this mindset, and you persevere, they will eventually move to a level of acceptance where the change becomes the "new normal," and the way things are done. At that point they'll begin resisting anything that will "change" the "new change."

   It's important that you recognize where people are in the cycle, and respond accordingly - or don't respond as we discussed in the section above - and allow them to move through the cycle on their own time frame as long as it doesn't impact yours. This cycle is illustrated below.

The Cycle of Resistance to Acceptance

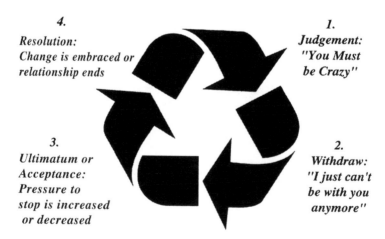

4.
Resolution:
Change is embraced or relationship ends

1.
Judgement:
"You Must be Crazy"

3.
Ultimatum or Acceptance:
Pressure to stop is increased or decreased

2.
Withdraw:
"I just can't be with you anymore"

5. **The more time you give to something – or someone – the more power it- or he/she has.**

   Resistance cannot be completely ignored but also can't become the main focus of your efforts. Focus on resistance instead of on leveraging the support you do have, and resistance is what you will have more of.

   So, the distinction here is to be aware of it, attempt to understand it, but don't let dealing with it take up all your time. Build on the support you have from others or you could lose them and be left with nothing but resistors.

6. **Although 100% support isn't required for a change to be successful, a critical mass of support is required.**

   You will always have a group of early adopters who will be on board for any change because it presents opportunities for something new and exciting. And, you will always have the group that will resist no matter what. Your focus must be on achieving the required critical mass by moving the in-between group from resistance to support. When you have converted a greater percentage of the detractors to your side and the tipping point to critical mass, you're home free.

7. **The key detractors give you the most headaches, but also teach you the most and have the potential to become your strongest advocates.**

   Remember that people resist change because they are in a self-protection mode. The reason they give you the most headaches may be that they are willing to verbalize the fears of others who aren't willing to speak up. Listen to what they say and realize that many others share their concerns as well.

   As we discussed in the last chapter, their resistance may be based on a "perceived" impact that makes sense to them but isn't visible or understandable to you. The earlier you can identify and deal with this, the greater the probability of success.

   The people that cause the most headaches also have the power to become your strongest advocates. If you can refocus their energy on how they can benefit from the change, and how important their support is to achieving success, they can become an advocate for your project instead of an advocate against your project.

8. **Leverage the power of the influence of others. You need a "peer" supporter in every group affected by the change.**

   Peers have influence that can be leveraged to work for you. As I mentioned earlier, you can spend a lot of time trying to get detractors on board when that time is better spent leveraging the influence of those who are up for the change. Build on the support of peers who may be in the "in-between" group and easier to convert to advocates who can influence others. We'll talk more about how to accomplish this in the next chapter on stakeholder engagement.

9. **Resistance is not a personal rejection of you**

   Don't create a "me against you" scenario. You have to be able to "rise above the resistance" and not take their reaction personally. It's not about you. It's all about their fears and concerns that are based on their interpretation of the outcome of your project.

   If you're preoccupied with protecting yourself from losing, you won't hear the concerns of others. If you are able to listen to and non-defensively respond to their concerns, you will be better prepared to nip resistance in the bud and turn resistors into advocates.

10. **Involving people in the process of change from the beginning generates the best outcome for everyone.**

    We don't resist what we create. We resist what we think we have no choice in bringing about. This is a very important distinction to keep in mind. Chances are that those affected by change will have better ideas about how to implement it than any leadership team will have anyway. The problem is, no one has bothered to ask them. If you do, you will cement their support.

    Involve those affected as much as possible in designing the future, that will become their future, and your probability of achieving and sustaining the benefits increases. Understand this, and you'll never have a problem implementing change.

11. **You are aiming for "Commitment" not "Compliance."**

    Compliance communicates "you must obey and have no choice." Being told to just accept change implies that an individual has no control over his or her future. Why wouldn't they resist? Remember, resistance is the only power people who see themselves as powerless have.

    Commitment, on the other hand, implies that you understand they have a choice and that they are CHOOSING to support your initiative. They are an "advocate" for the change and not a "victim" of the change. You are asking for their commitment not their compliance.

    To reinforce what was stated in Principle 10, involvement in creating the solution increases a sense of owning the outcome rather than being a "victim" of the outcome. This lessens the need to resist to feel powerful.

12. **We all want to be heard and respected for our beliefs. Resistance reflects our belief that what is happening should not be happening, or should not be happening the way it is happening.**

    We want someone to listen to us and acknowledge that we could possibly be right - or at least have an idea about how things could be done better. We don't want to be treated like children who just don't understand what the "right" answer is. I've found that if you treat individuals like children, they will behave like children.

    As badly as you want to convince someone that your way is the "right way," you have to accept the reality that they can – and will – make their own assessment of what is the "right way" and the" wrong way" and will behave accordingly.

    Treat others with a level of respect that reflects the professionals they are. Acknowledge that they have the experience and understanding of the current environment to make recommendations on the best approach to take to successfully implement change. After all, they're living with it every day.

Application of the Twelve Basic Principles

Cynthia came into our next meeting looking a little less dejected. "So, tell me what you're thinking our next steps should be to turn Hans back into an advocate," I asked.

I find that it's important to focus on what we will do rather than talk in general terms about what we could do.

But, I think Cynthia was expecting a little more of a sympathetic ear from me and less of an attitude of "let's move on and get this done." However, I was concerned that if we didn't turn the Twelve Basic Principles into actions she could take immediately with the Steering Team, she would think they were only theories with no practical application in the real world.

"I read and reread the Twelve Basic Principles you gave me," she responded. "I can see how I have reacted defensively to people in the past who didn't agree with me or who I believed were slowing me down and preventing me from getting things done. But, I've been rewarded for getting things done and not for taking time to understand what people are thinking or feeling. I can see the benefit of trying a different approach but it's difficult for me to see that it won't take up more of my time with no guarantee of a better outcome. Especially, she emphasized, since I'll be rewarded for getting this project done on time and on budget."

I listened closely to what she was saying because it told me that any suggestion I made to Cynthia had to be positioned in a way that would address her concern of slowing the project down. Otherwise, it would be rejected.

"Cynthia," I responded, "you have to have these conversations anyway. You have to interact with people on the project on a regular basis. We're not talking about creating more work. What we're talking about is refocusing. You're replacing old words and behaviors that haven't worked with ones that will be less defensive and more effective in building support."

"Refocusing requires learning to use what I call "focused" listening to understand what is really going on. Focused listening is non-defensive listening where your intention is to *learn* and not to *defend*. This takes some practice before it becomes your natural behavior, but you'll find that the results are worth the effort," I concluded.

"So give me some examples," a no-nonsense Cynthia responded. "I want to know exactly what to say and what not to say, and what to do and what not do, so I can get this done and move on."

"As we've talked about," I began, "people often feel threatened during times of change and communicate in a defensive manner to protect themselves from loss – real or perceived. Your effectiveness in leading people through change can be greatly enhanced by learning to identify and respond to defensive behavior. We're going to use the information below to craft a way to respond to Hans and learn techniques for communicating with other members of the Steering Team and in the larger organization to turn resistors into advocates."

Cynthia and I reviewed the tables below that describe the difference between defensive and non-defensive communication

To make this exercise real and not theoretical, I asked Cynthia to identify people on the Steering Team who exhibited behaviors in the left hand column at the last meeting.

DEFENSIVE BEHAVIOR	**NON-DEFENSIVE RESPONSE**
Intent: To Protect	**Intent: To Learn**
➢ Silence	➢ What's the perceived or real loss?
➢ Withdraw	➢ How can we work together to work this out?
➢ Attack	➢ How could this benefit both of us?

"They were all in the left column," she replied. "Once we started talking about the impact they didn't say anything – with the exception of Hans who went on the attack and Charles who supported him."

"And what did you do?" I asked. "Which column describes your behavior?"

"I attacked back, she responded."

"And how well did that work for us," I asked?

"Not very well," she responded. "But tell me what I was supposed to do? When you're attacked you attack back!"

Refocus Resistance

"You're right. And, that's what gets you stuck in the resistance," I responded.

"You reacted defensively because you were reacting to the threat of your project being slowed down," I explained. "You reacted from the intent to protect rather than from the intent to learn. The meeting ended in a stalemate because everyone else withdrew when you and Hans started attacking each other. I wonder if the outcome could have been different if you had responded with the intent to learn described in the right hand column. Would this have allowed us to have a productive conversation that focused on a solution rather than one that kept us focusing on the objections? If so, we could have saved time because we wouldn't have needed this additional meeting to start the discussion all over again."

I paused after this last statement. There are times when silence can be very effective.

"Let's look at what we can do to refocus the conversation in our meeting with Hans, and in our next Steering Committee meeting, that will allow you to move forward with your project and stay on schedule," I replied.

"I have 30 minutes," Cynthia responded. "Let's come up with a plan."

Non-Defensive Communication = Lower Resistance

"Step one is to determine if the resistance you're hearing is based on facts, beliefs, and feelings or in conflict with someone's values. Once you understand the source then you can respond more effectively and possibly nip resistance in the bud – so to speak. Let's look at the table below to determine what we believe Han's response was based on," I suggested.

Source of Their Argument	Objective of Your Response
1. Facts	Verify the facts
2. Beliefs	Challenge the beliefs
3. Feelings	Address the typical feelings of fear and anger
4. Values	Relate change to what they believe is important

"It was based on the fact that his area will experience a greater impact from the project and will have to make more changes." Cynthia responded.

"That's correct," I said, "and it was also based on his belief that the changes weren't needed and the concern that his area couldn't handle it."

"I guess it was all of that," Cynthia responded.

"So, if we look at the right hand column we can say that we did verify the facts, we did challenge his belief that the changes weren't necessary but we didn't convince him. We did not acknowledge his feelings and we didn't connect the value of the project to the benefit he originally believed this project would bring to the company overall. Is that an accurate assessment,?" I asked Cynthia.

"Although I didn't realize it at the time," she responded, "I believe it is."

"So at our next meeting," I suggested, "we'll want to listen to his objections, reconfirm the facts about the impact to his area as we understand it today, and refocus his thinking on the value he believes this project will bring to the company."

"Since he has been one of the most vocal advocates, it's difficult for him to back down now that he's learned his area will experience the greatest impact. Also, remember that one of the Twelve Principles was to leverage the influence of peers, I don't think that Han's peers on the Steering Committee will allow him to back down, since he was one of the most vocal when many of them didn't want this project to continue."

"That's a really good point," Cynthia replied. "I think I'm beginning to see how applying the principles may help."

This is starting to go in a better direction I thought.

"We also have to address his fears that his area won't be able to handle the change and refocus on what we can do to lessen that concern and make sure they are prepared," I continued.

"OK, I'm following so far. Just tell me what to say", Cynthia replied

"Well, there isn't a script for you to memorize," I began. " Your response has to be in your own words. What we've talked about so far is understanding the reasons that people resist, recognizing defensive behavior, and identifying the reason for their reaction. We can then engage in a more effective dialogue that is focused on achieving our goals by including them in a solution, instead of arguing with their objections and making them feel wrong, powerless, or out of control."

"That was also addressed in the Twelve Principles," Cynthia replied.

Refocus Resistance

It felt good that she was beginning to understand the realistic application of the Twelve Principles in the real world and not just think of them as consulting theory.

"The table below that suggests possible responses that may help you come up with your own. Why don't you take time to read over this information and map out the key points you want to make in our meeting with Hans?" I suggested. "Again, this has to be your own words and not a memorized script," I emphasized.

"Once you understand how to respond to cause of resistance," I continued, " knowing what to say won't be difficult. It's basically the 'yes and' response referred to in one of the Twelve Principles that refocuses on agreements instead of objections. It makes it easier to include them in the solution, and gives them a feeling of being more in control of the situation."

Argument	Your Response…Yes, and…
No need for change	Explain why the change is necessary and how the changes will allow them to better meet their needs.
Change is seen as a threat	Defuse the threat by correcting inaccurate information or assumptions and stressing benefits. Ask for their suggestions on alternatives that could be more effective.
Risks outweigh the benefits	Discuss perceived risks to correct inaccurate information or mistaken beliefs. Ask for their suggestions on how to minimize the risk.
Goal can be achieved without making changes	Provide facts about current conditions of the organization and its competition. Explain how the change will help the organization survive and grow
Supports change but doesn't like the approach	Listen, avoid making excuses (yes, but) and ask for advice on a better approach to use to implement this or future changes
The change will fail	Let them know that their help is needed to make the change successful. Ask for their suggestions on what to do to increase the probability of success and their support in doing this.

"This is helpful," Cynthia responded
  "I'm glad," I replied.

"Another skill that is beneficial is to learn to listen 'between the lines.' As mentioned in the Twelve Principles, the words we use don't often reflect how we really feel, and our behaviors don't match our words. Let's work through the exercise below to begin to understand how to listen between the lines to hear what people are really saying."

When you're hearing...	What they're really saying is...
"We've tried that here before."	"I've been able to stop it once and I'll stop it again." or "It didn't work before so why would it work now?"
"I support this idea one hundred percent, but there are a lot of people around here who don't."	"I don't support it either. I just want you to think I do."
"I'm completely in favor of this change, but my group is different. I don't think it will work here."	"It's not going to be my fault if it doesn't work." or "And, I'll make sure it doesn't"
"I like the idea, but the timing is too fast. I think we need to slow this down and do it in more controlled phases."	"I'm not ready."

"So, it's pretty uncomfortable to think that I always have to question if people mean what they say. Can't I believe what anyone says?" Cynthia asked.

"Of course," I replied. " It's when their behavior doesn't match the words that this skill comes in handy. It can be really confusing when people are saying they're supportive, but their actions don't back that up. Plus, they're often blaming others, instead of admitting that what they're saying other people are thinking or feeling really reflects what they're thinking or feeling. This is the hidden resistance that is more difficult to deal with. On the surface everything appears great, but the reality is that nothing happens that moves you toward achieving your goal."

"I'm beginning to think that the focused listening will be one of the most valuable skills I can learn," Cynthia responded.

"You're probably right." I replied

Refocus Resistance

The "Got You" Game Resistors Play

"Another key communication skill I want to help you develop is how to respond to blame and the "got-you" game that you may encounter when people are communicating defensively."

"When defensiveness is expressed as blame, it's difficult not to respond back by either attacking or accepting the blame - even though you're not responsible. It's important to be able to identify when this is happening and to refocus your communication toward a solution and not allow it to continue on a win/lose path."

"The table below lists what you may hear and possible responses you can use that will help you avoid 'taking the bait' and refocus the conversation in the direction you need it to go."

When You Hear…	You Can Respond With…
"Prove it!" "Convince me that the outcome will be something I want to live with. "	"What would it take to convince you?"
"Since I'm not the only one who thinks this project is crazy, you really are crazy to be doing this." "He said/she said….." "Everybody says…."	"Thank you for letting me know. This provides a wonderful opportunity for us to have a meeting with anyone – and everyone - who thinks this so you and I can explain the benefits."
"You are responsible for the situation I find myself in." "It's all your fault."	"Do you really believe I'm that powerful and capable of doing something like this all by myself?"
"You have to!" "I'm in control. I tell you what you can and cannot do."	"I see other options, such as….."
"I can't do this myself." "Fix it for me."	"I have every confidence you can. Let's meet tomorrow and discuss what you can do."
"No one's ever done anything like this."	"That's interesting. Let's focus on what we are doing." "We all have our strengths and weaknesses."

Silence	Interpret the silence: "Your silence is telling me that you have no objections and fully support what I'm doing"
"Everyone agrees with me and thinks you're wrong."	"Everybody?" "Could you be more specific about what's wrong?"
"Surely you're smart enough to realize this is totally unacceptable." "Even you should ….."	"I'm sure that wasn't what you meant to say." "You probably weren't aware of how that sounded."
"You're not listening."	"I heard what you said, (repeat what was said) however, I see it this way…"

"Wow, that's a lot to remember," Cynthia responded. "Am I supposed to take this list with me every time I talk to someone about this project?" Cynthia asked very defensively.

"No," I replied. "My advice is to try one response, or apply one technique and see how it works. You have to apply it before it becomes real or has any chance of working."

"I think I can do this," she replied tentatively.

"I think you can too," I replied. I was beginning to feel much more optimistic than I had the day before.

"If you can begin to recognize when you're being defensive and instead refocus on hearing what is really going on with the other person, you can begin to work with them on a possible solution they can support instead of resist. It won't be long before you will have adopted a new way of interacting with others that will seem natural. Besides, I'm here to help you. And, Hans has provided you with a wonderful opportunity to learn what does and doesn't work when talking about change."

"Great," Cynthia replied. "That's a learning opportunity I really didn't want!"

Application in the "Real" World

Our meeting with Hans took place the next day. I was very proud of the way Cynthia began the discussion by saying "Hans, your support of the project from the very beginning has meant so much to me. You've been our most vocal advocate. At our last meeting it seemed that all that changed. So many people look up to you and trust what you say. I wanted to have this meeting with you to understand more about the concerns you have that brought that change about."

"Cynthia," Hans replied, "no one in the US understands how difficult it is for us to continue to hear that we're the ones who have to change. I fully understand and support the benefits we'll all experience as a result of this project. I continue to strongly believe that it's the best move for the company to make. It just feels like the US makes the decisions and we're expected to agree. It's very much of a "decide and announce" approach to dealing with us. Since we're the ones who are contributing 75% of the profits of this company, maybe - just maybe - we have better ideas about how to get things done that could be beneficial to this project."

"When I heard yesterday about the changes we're expected to make while the US can continue with their less efficient processes," Hans continued, "it was the tipping point for me. I thought the one power I had left was the power to say 'no!' we will not do this. And, that's what I did!"

"Your reaction is understandable," Cynthia responded. "Europe has had very little involvement in the decision-making process to date, and that needs to change. Can we talk about how we might be able to take a different approach on this project so we don't repeat the mistakes of the past?"

To say I was amazed would be an understatement. Cynthia did her homework. She approached Hans in a non-defensive way with the intent to learn what was really going on with him instead of the intent to protect herself and her project by either attacking him for disagreeing in the meeting, or ignoring the issue he expressed and attempting to move forward without his support. Her approach acknowledge his concerns, validated his feelings and made him part of the solution instead of the problem.

"Just exactly how do you propose doing that?" Hans questioned a little cautiously.

"Well, that's what we have Rita for, "Cynthia responded.

Targeted Engagement Refocuses Resistance

In the next chapter you'll read how we went about developing a Stakeholder Engagement Plan that gave Hans and his group a voice in creating their future, increased their feeling of being in control of their future, and refocused their resistance to put them back in the position of being our strongest advocates.

Manager's Quick Guide to Achieving Change Readiness

1. Resistance is not about you. Change is interpreted through the lens of WIMFM (what it means for me). What you see as exciting someone else may see as threatening. Be sensitive to the fact that your gain may result in someone else's loss.

    a. *Resistance may not make sense to you but it makes sense to the person who is resisting. Understand the basis for their resistance and you'll know how to communicate non-defensively to address real or perceived concerns*

    b. *Resistance can be expressed verbally or through behavior. It's important to pay attention to both, especially when someone's behavior does not reflect their verbal expression of support.*

2. 100% support is not a requirement for success.

    a. *You will have people who embrace change as an existing new opportunity and those that resist change for reasons that are valid to them.*

    b. *Leverage the 20% who initially support change to convert those who fall in the "in-between" group to become change advocates. You will have the critical mass required for success and the 20% who resist no matter what, will not have the power to stop you.*

3. The loudest resistors can become your strongest advocates if you are able to refocus their energy from blocking the change to "owning" the change.

    a. *Resistance is power used by those who feel powerless. Redirect the power of resistors who are critical stakeholders to work with you not against you.*

    b. *If they feel that they are a part of what is happening, they are less likely to feel and behave like a victim of what is happening and support rather than sabotage your project.*

Change Readiness Thinking

Keep the following in mind to shift your thinking to a Change Readiness Mindset

1. Be clear and consistent in your communication. You lose credibility and increase resistance when you send mixed messages. Deal with the truth and communicate honestly about what will change, and the benefits and losses that will result from the change..
2. Become an objective listener. Remember that resistance is not about you. Respond to resistance by trying to learn about their fears instead of defending (protecting) yourself.
3. If you argue with objections - objections become the focus. Describing a situation is a good communication skill to use to avoid attacking an individual. Acknowledge – don't ignore - their feelings. Sometimes, that's all that's needed to reduce resistance
4. Work toward resolution - not victory. Focus on fixing the problem not the blame. You want commitment not compliance. Don't be afraid to admit you don't have all the answers.
5. Insist on appropriate behavior. What is rewarded is repeated. Ask yourself how you may be rewarding the people who are resistance by focusing more attention on them than the ones who are your advocates. Remember that what you give time to, you give power to.
6. You get people to do what you want them to do not by tricking or bullying them, but by understanding them.

CHAPTER 4
ENGAGE STAKEHOLDERS EFFECTIVELY

"I need to feel needed to feel secure"

I was pleased that the conversation between Hans and Cynthia had gone so well. It opened the door to discussing the criticality of effective communication and stakeholder engagement in building change readiness for the project and change ready capability in the organization.

In Chapter 2 we defined "stakeholder" as anyone who can affect or will be affected by the outcome of your change initiative. A stakeholder is someone who has the power to influence the outcome by providing or withholding their support, as well as someone whose life will change in some way as a result of your project.

Critical Stakeholders are individuals who have a greater degree of influence or who will experience a greater change impact from your initiative.

As discussed in Chapter 3, communication and engagement are key steps in turning resistors to advocates. It's also important to understand the difference between communicating and engaging, when communication alone is sufficient, when engagement is indicated and how to develop a plan for doing both effectively to achieve change readiness.

The Stakeholder Engagement Plan defines the process for effectively engaging stakeholders in a way that allows them to take ownership of the outcome rather than see themselves as "victims" of the outcome of a change initiative.

> *Although a Communication Plan is a key component of a Stakeholder Engagement Plan, communication alone isn't sufficient to gain the level of commitment required from critical stakeholders to execute a successful project and sustain benefits for the organization.*

The goal of communication is to create awareness by providing accurate and timely information. Regular communication is needed throughout the project. Key messages can be consistent company-wide or tailored to address specific concerns of different audiences.

The goals of engagement are to increase understanding, build alignment and create a sense of ownership of the change among people who will live with the results of the change. In this chapter we will define the factors that determine the type of stakeholder engagements that will be most effective in achieving change readiness.

Involvement = Ownership = Commitment

We don't resist what we create. The more involved someone is in a project, the more they will feel a sense of ownership of the outcome and the greater their commitment will be to seeing it succeed.

An effective Stakeholder Engagement Plan is tailored to achieve the degree of involvement indicated by the level of stakeholder influence and impact. The greater the influence or impact, the more involved you want your stakeholders to be.

The purpose of the Impact Analysis we discussed in Chapter 2 is to begin the process of identifying critical stakeholders based on their level of influence and impact

As I explained to Hans and Cynthia, different levels of involvement will be required from different stakeholder groups throughout a project.

And, as the Stakeholder Influence/Impact Involvement approach described in the section that follows illustrates, these support levels fall along a continuum, from awareness to ownership of the project's success.

I began my conversation with Hans and Cynthia by reviewing the Stakeholder Influence/Impact Involvement Scale. My goal was to help them understand how we could use this tool to guide us in developing a Stakeholder Engagement Plan that would provide opportunities for Europe to be more involved in this project than they had been in past projects.

Since Hans was the Senior Director of European Operations, he was very interested in learning how we could do this.

Application of Stakeholder Engagement Model

I explained to Cynthia and Hans that we could use the Stakeholder Impact/Involvement Model to plot where the stakeholder groups fall on the low, medium and high impact scale on the graph and define our engagement objective. I pointed out the following:

1. The scale illustrates the appropriate level of stakeholder involvement based on their level of influence and impact.
2. The word in each oval defines the objective of each stakeholder group's involvement.
3. The quotation beside each oval describes the level of understanding and commitment that is the desired outcome at this level of involvement.

"Hans," I began, "as Director of European Operations, you fall into the high influence category because of your position and also into the high impact category since your area will experience the biggest change impact from the project. Looking at our graph we can see that this indicates an "ownership" level of involvement. Our engagement objective for you, and others who fall into this category, is to achieve the highest level of commitment and an attitude toward the project of 'I will do what it takes to make it happen'."

Engage Stakeholders Effectively

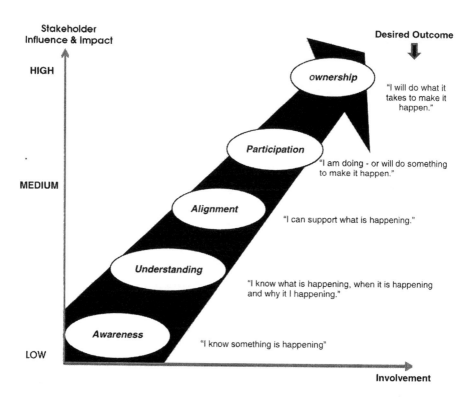

"We can only achieve this objective by making sure that you are fully informed, involved and agree to own the outcome of this project in Europe. Ownership of the outcome requires that we define a role for you that includes responsibility for ensuring that Europe is prepared for, and able to sustain, the changes they will experience."

"Regina Dion, on the other hand, is an influencer because of her position as the Senior Director of Canadian Operations. Since her area will experience very little change from this project, they fall lower on the impact scale. Because of this, we only need to involve her at the awareness and understanding level on the engagement scale. We'll keep her informed, but we won't need to engage her as often or to as great an extent as we will you and Charles and others in Europe who will experience the greatest change."

"Also," I pointed out, "it annoys people when you inundate them with information that doesn't affect them. After a while they stop paying attention and begin ignoring the information you really want them to have. On the other hand, they feel left out if they aren't provided with updates about what is happening. We have to strike a balance between the two extremes. This model can help us do that and ensure that people have the right information and the right involvement at the right time, so that we achieve our objectives."

"Let's continue with this exercise to plot where your direct reports fall on the scale. Hans, you will need buy-in from your managers and from their direct reports to have a successful rollout and to sustain benefits in each area. You can't do this completely by yourself," I emphasized.

"Since large-scale change can only be successful if it is addressed on an individual basis at the local level, you have to leverage the skills and relationships of your managers and supervisors - who are closest to the employees who must adopt a new way of working - for this initiative to be successful. Whether from a geographic, reporting or relationship perspective, they have greater influence on how well their employees understand, embrace and are prepared for the change."

"Also", I continued, " we have to keep in mind that your managers not only have to prepare their people for change, they also are going to be affected personally by this initiative. They have a dual role as a recipient of the change and a leader of the change. How they do their job will change also. They have to be prepared to deal with their own change while preparing their employees for change. Their role as a change ready leader is critical to our success. "

"Once we determine the desired level of involvement we need from your managers, based on impact to themselves and their area, we will want to meet with them and continue this process through the supervisory level. We'll then be able to categorize our high, medium and low impact groups in Europe and develop an engagement plan that achieves our change readiness objectives with each group "

"I like this model," Han's responded. "We should discuss this at our next Steering Committee Meeting and ask for each Steering Committee Member to follow the same process in his or her area."

"That is exactly what we need to do," I responded. "And," I cautiously but optimistically continued, "it would be great if you could co-present this model to the Steering Committee with us. Plus, we will want you, as

Senior Director of European Operations, to introduce this to your leadership team so they know that you support this process and that you need and expect them to be involved in the project."

"I will be happy to do both," Hans responded.

"That's great!" a surprised Cynthia responded. I think she was amazed that we had not only been able to address Han's resistance, we had also been successful in obtaining his support of our approach and his ownership of next steps of presenting to his peers on the Steering Committee and to his direct reports in Europe.

If you look back at some of the techniques described in Chapter 3 on turning resistors into advocates, you'll have a better understanding of how we did this.

"Rita," she continued," what do we do next?"

"First," I responded, "we'll present this approach at the Steering Committee to gain their understanding and agreement to do the same with their direct reports as Han's as agreed to do with his. Our goal is to achieve full agreement. However, if you remember one of the Twelve Principles for Responding to Resistance, we don't need agreement from everyone to move forward. We do need agreement from a critical mass. We'll move forward and begin working with the next level of management in the areas where we do have agreement from their Steering Team representative to do this. Hopefully, the peer pressure from those who support this approach will influence those who don't initially to get on board."

"We'll then be ready to begin engaging stakeholders at the lower levels by establishing a Cross-Functional Change Network that will include representatives from each high impact area. Their role will be to serve as a liaison between the project and employees in the area they represent to do the following:

1. Provide regular and consistent project updates
2. Answer questions and address concerns
3. Escalate issues to the Executive Steering Team that could block success on the local level.
4. Serve as a mentor to ensure that people are prepared and ready to implement and sustain the change after the project ends.

The benefit of taking this approach cascades involvement and ownership throughout the organization and greatly increases the probability of achieving change that will last. In addition, it creates an opportunity to develop change ready skills throughout the organization that will serve you well now and with future projects."

"Of course we will need the support of management to be able to do this. That will be one of our objectives when we meet with the middle manager and supervisory levels of high-impact areas"

"That sounds great," Cynthia responded, "but also sounds like it will take a lot of time and a lot of resources. I'm not sure we can get support for that."

"I agree," Hans replied, "our people are overworked as it is. Adding on more responsibilities to what they're already doing won't go over very well. This will take a lot of convincing with my managers as well as with other Steering Committee members."

I wasn't surprised or discouraged by their reaction. As we discussed in Chapter 3 on Refocusing Resistance:

People often agree with an idea until they understand what putting it into action actually entails.

Han's and Cynthia's objections provided an opportunity for me to apply some of the principles of responding to resistance, I had explained to Cynthia, that we would need to follow continually throughout the project.

"I understand the challenge," I responded. "We'll present a well thought out plan so others will see this as an investment of resources that will produce the desired ROI because the organization will be better prepared to accept, execute and sustain change. Also, by being involved in executing the change, employees will learn change readiness skills they can apply to other projects. After all, this won't be the last change initiative this company launches."

"That's certainly true," they both responded with a nervous laugh.

"After we take another look at the Impact Analysis we recently completed, and update our Stakeholder Analysis" I continued, "we'll have a better understanding of the level of involvement we'll need throughout the organization. We'll be in a better position to establish a case for the number of resources needed and time requirements."

"For now, let's be prepared to present the Stakeholder Impact/Involvement Model and the Three Tiered Stakeholder Engagement process that we'll review next, to better understand the roles and responsibilities of each level and gain understanding and support for the approach I just described."

"We have to remember that introducing the concept of change readiness and working to develop a 'change ready' culture in your organization is a *change*,' " I pointed out. "So, to be successful, we also have to follow the change models we're introducing."

"I hadn't really thought about it that way," Cynthia responded," but you're absolutely right. I've been resistant to this whole idea of change readiness myself."

"You and a few others," Hans replied with a smile.

"That's quite understandable," I replied. "Plus, your reactions will give you a better understanding of what others are likely to feel and how they may respond to our recommendations."

Three Tiered Organizational Involvement Approach

Following the three Tiered Organizational Involvement process ensures that the three tiers of employee, managers and senior executives are informed, involved as appropriate and prepared for the changes that will occur.

It provides a framework for defining the role and responsibilities of key stakeholder groups who need to "own" change readiness for a successful implementation and sustainment of the changes to occur.

I used this framework to explain to Hans and Cynthia the role and responsibilities of the three levels of the organization in ensuring a successful execution of our current project.

"As we had discussed earlier," I began, "a stakeholder's level of involvement should be proportional to the role he or she plays in the success of the change. However, **how** they're involved, as well as the role and responsibilities they are asked to take on, needs to be clearly defined and agreed to. If not, you will only create a forum for people to express opinions about what should happen, or criticize what is happening, instead of doing something themselves to achieve a successful outcome."

It's the action stakeholders take that provides the level of involvement they need to create an individual feeling of ownership of the outcome. Remember, we don't resist what we create.

I also used the 3 Tiered Framework to introduce the concept of developing change readiness capabilities among leadership and the opportunity to use this project to begin developing change readiness skills throughout the organization that would create a change ready culture.

"An additional benefit of the Three Tiered Organizational Framework," I continued, "is that it creates a centralized-decentralized approach for building support and achieving change readiness throughout the organization. It allows tailoring to meet specific needs but also ensures quality through following a consistent approach."

"The centralized approach achieves consistency across the organization through the use of standardized plans, tools, and templates and consistently defined roles."

"It also supports a *decentralized* deployment of change readiness activities at the local level that allows customizing these activities to the needs and cultural differences of each area. This is an important benefit because it promotes local ownership for change readiness."

Everybody has a Role in Making Change Successful.

Let's take a closer look at each of the three enterprise-wide stakeholder groups to understand their responsibilities and how they will need to be prepared to take on the change readiness role.

Executive Steering Team

The senior leader of each area affected by the project should be a member of the Executive Steering Team and assume the role of "Change Sponsor" for the area they represent. As the results of the IBM Study, referred to in Chapter Two revealed, the active involvement by senior leaders as a visible and vocal sponsor of change is a major contributor to overall project success.

Engage Stakeholders Effectively

The table below outlines the role of senior leadership and requirements for successful execution of the role throughout the project.

Executive Role and Responsibilities

There are three primary responsibilities for executives and senior managers in the role of Change Sponsors:
1. Play an active and visible role throughout the project.
2. Build a coalition of sponsorship and manage resistance from their peers.
3. Communicate clearly and directly with employees.

In order for them to be successful in this role, they will need concrete examples of the specific actions you ask them to take. Basically, a "to-do" list. Make it as easy as possible for them to be great sponsors by:
a. Doing the legwork (create talking points, write communication, prepare presentations).
b. Leveraging meetings they already attend to minimize the time they are asked to give to the project. Remember, they already have a pretty significant fulltime job.

Don't forget to thank them for their involvement and let them know what a difference it makes. Again, everybody needs to be needed and to have their efforts acknowledged.

Middle Managers and Supervisors

This is the group most often overlooked but the most critical to building change readiness.

Managers are affected by change personally as well as being responsible for preparing their employees for change. If the manager has a change ready attitude, the employees will also.

Many times, the supervisory and middle management levels aren't in a position to make decisions about the project and may not have been involved in discussions about the feasibility of doing the project. They have only been told to make it happen.

This, of course, creates a breeding ground for resistance to develop and grow. And, as we learned in Chapter 3, resistance is the "power of the powerless" and often the only option individuals see as a way to regain control over their future.

As I discussed with Hans, middle managers and supervisors are the closest to those employees who must adopt and sustain change for the expected benefits to be realized. Because they are instrumental in creating an environment where the change will either be seen as a change for the better or a change for the worse, we need this group to be our key ally in building change readiness across the organization. Employees will look to their immediate supervisor for an indication of what lies ahead.

*If you have the support of middle managers and supervisors,
you will have the support of their employees*

The involvement of managers and supervisors also helps you maximize change readiness activities to achieve large-scale change. If each manager assumes responsibility for ensuring that their employees understand what is changing, why it is changing, how they will be affected, and how they will be prepared, you will have an entire organization that is ready to launch and sustain your change initiative.

It's important to clearly define the roles and responsibilities of managers and supervisors so they understand what they need to do and to ensure consistency in the approach managers follow across the organization.

The Manager Role and Responsibilities Table outlines the role of managers and supervisors as Change Readiness Leaders and what is required to prepare them to perform this role.

> **Manager Role and Responsibilities**
> There are five primary roles for managers and supervisors as Change Readiness Leaders:
> 1. Communicator
> 2. Advocate
> 3. Coach
> 4. Liaison
> 5. Resistance Minimizer
>
> In order for them to be successful in this role they will need to:
>
> a. Have their boss acknowledge the importance of their role and also reinforce accountability for a successful launch in their area by including this responsibility in their performance objectives
>
> b. Understand the benefits and impact of the change and be able to explain it to their employees
>
> c. Have accurate and timely information on the initiative so they can communicate effectively with their direct reports
>
> d. Be given an opportunity to voice their concerns and objections so they feel that they have been heard and will no longer have a reason to resist.
>
> e. Understand the techniques for turning resistors into advocates outlined in Chapter Three so that they can support their direct reports, as well as deal with their own fears, during the transition process.

Conducting Change Leadership Workshops for managers is an effective way to teach them change leadership skills and to work with them to tailor a Change Readiness Plan for their area. We'll talk more about this in Chapter 5 on preparation.

Change Readiness Team

The Change Readiness Team is a cross-functional group of non-management representatives from each function, department, job role and/or region affected by the project.

Members of the Change Readiness Team serve as your "eyes and ears" into the organization. They provide you with valuable information about how the project is being perceived in their area and what the local issues and concerns are that, if not addressed, can prevent you from being successful.

Their primary role is to inform and prepare their co-workers for change. Since change is managed most effectively on a local level, their involvement is critical to your success. As we learned in Chapter Three:

> *Leveraging the influence of peers is key to*
> *overcoming resistance and building support.*

The Change Readiness Team meets on a regular basis and provides a forum for a two-way flow of communication and feedback from the project to the areas they represent.

Employees at this level often only know what their managers have told them about the purpose, benefits and impact of a project. If their manager has had little involvement or information they will have had even less. If their manager is resistant they will be even more so.

> *Lack of information creates an opportunity for people*
> *to make up a worst case scenario about change.*

Being a member of a Change Readiness Team or Change Network provides an opportunity for them to be "in-the-know" about what's happening and increases their sense of importance to the project and benefit to the company.

Their involvement builds readiness, reduces resistance, and allows you to become aware of potential issues at the local level before they become risks to the project. It also provides a foundation to build change readiness capability throughout the organization.

The value of a cross-functional Change Readiness Team in achieving change readiness and sustaining the benefits of change in an organization cannot be underestimated.

Change Readiness Team Role and Responsibilities

Members of a Change Readiness Team are often referred to as "Change Champions," "Change Liaisons" "Change Agents," or "SPOCS" (single points of contact). The role of the Change Readiness Team is to facilitate the execution of change in an organization by performing the following activities:

1. Communicating project goals and status to their peers
2. Building relationships across functions and regions
3. Providing feedback to the project about how the project is being perceived
4. Identifying organizational risks that could prevent a successful rollout in their area
5. Defining success and readiness criteria for the area they represent
6. Identifying training needs and the most effective training methods for their area
7. Serving as mentors and "go-to" experts after launch to sustain the change

In order to be prepared to fulfill these responsibilities they will need to be:

a. Supported by their manager and respected by their peers
b. Recognized for the process, regional or functional expertise they bring to the team

> c. Aware of how their involvement as a member of the team bridges the organizational "silos" and contributes to the cross-functional "one-team mindset" required for the successful roll-out of a change initiative.
> d. Trained on change readiness methodology, tools and processes
> e. Provided with change management templates for communication, assessment and training activities and on-going coaching from a change management professional on the execution of the tools and activities
> f. Informed about the overall project plan and understand the change readiness milestones that are integrated with and support the project milestones
> g. Rewarded for this role by including in performance goals

Reconfirming Agreement

"Is what I've described with both the Stakeholder Engagement and Three Tier Organizational Involvement Framework an approach that you both feel comfortable with and can support?" I asked.

"I think it sounds like a good first step," Hans replied.

"I'm ok Rita," Cynthia responded, "as long as you're the one who presents it."

"I'll pull the presentation together and schedule a time to review with both of you," I replied. "We'll each need to play a role in the presentation to show a united front."

"Hans, since we have your support to move forward with your organization, I would like to draft an email for you to send to each of your direct reports explaining that I will be scheduling a meeting with each one of them to discuss the project and the role we will be asking them to play to help us be successful."

I wanted to confirm that we had agreement from Hans to move forward, in spite of his concerns about time and resource requirements. I also wanted to know that we had been successful in achieving our goal of

Engage Stakeholders Effectively

reducing his resistance and increasing his involvement and ownership of a successful outcome in Europe.

I was happy to hear Han's reply: "let's get the ball rolling."

When to Communicate and When to Engage

After we left our meeting with Hans, Cynthia replied, "this is a lot more complicated than I realized. I thought having a Communication Plan would be enough. You know, just send a few emails now and then."

"You aren't alone in thinking that Cynthia," I responded. "That's the approach that way too many projects take and one reason why there is such a high failure rate for change initiatives. Project leaders often think that if they've communicated, they've 'done' change management."

If the change is significant enough to require people to learn new skills, do their work in a different way or adopt a new mindset that differs from the current culture, communication alone just isn't enough. Engaging stakeholders is the most effective method for minimizing resistance and building readiness

"Cynthia," I continued, "it's important to understand the difference between communicating with stakeholders and engaging stakeholders, and to develop a plan that defines objectives and a timeline for each one."

"Since we'll need both for this project, let's talk a little more about how they're different, and how we'll go about developing each one."

"An Engagement Plan defines how to involve key stakeholders at key points throughout the project to build change readiness. It provides you with a timeline to follow that will achieve the level of involvement required to meet the engagement objective for that stakeholder group."

"An effective Communication Plan provides you with the structure and tools to provide accurate and consistent information to people on a regular basis to help you dispel rumors, correct misperceptions and misinformation, lessen confusion and reduce resistance throughout the project."

"When people don't have information, they make it up. What they "make up" is much worse than the reality of what the change is all about. This results in resistance that is based on misunderstanding."

"A Communication Plan can minimize this by providing consistent key messages and regular updates across the organization."

"Stakeholder engagement sessions provide a forum to do this in smaller groups, or one-on-one, and an opportunity to employ the techniques and methods we've discussed for communicating non-defensively to minimize resistance," I concluded.

I reviewed the following components of an effective Communication Plan with Cynthia so she would have an increased level of understanding and confidence to support Hans when they presented our recommended Stakeholder Engagement and Communication Plans to the Executive Steering Team.

Communication and Engagement Plan Overview

Although communication is the responsibility of everyone on a project and a key responsibility for Sponsors, Change Readiness Leaders and the Change Readiness Team as we defined earlier, every project will need someone to "own" communication. The size and scope of the project will determine whether a full-time or part-time resource is needed to execute the plan and monitor its effectiveness.

An effective Communication Plan is tailored to achieve the required level of awareness and support from each target audience and typically includes the following components:

1. **Communication Schedule** to provide information that people need when they need it.
2. **One and Two Way Communication Tools** that serve as channels for continuous communication and feedback processes.
3. **Guidelines for Defining Key Messages and Materials** that are tailored to meet the objectives of the current phase of the project or address the concerns of a specific audience.

Engage Stakeholders Effectively

4. **Key Metrics** for evaluating communication effectiveness to confirm that the communication objectives with each audience are being achieved.

Examples of each item listed above is included in the section below

Communication Schedule

A communication plan can be developed in different formats but typically contains the information in the example below.

Audience	Objective	Message	Method	Distribution Date	Approval Date	Owner	Feedback

The schedule can be completed by month, per stakeholder group, region or department for larger projects, as well as enterprise-wide for the entire project. The key steps are to:

1. Identify the communication audience:

   Who is the recipient of the message?

2. Define the objective and key message:

   What do you want them to know?

3. Select the method:

   What is the best tool to use to relay this information?

4. Define the roles:

   Who needs to approve, distribute and own the process?

5. Document feedback:

   How will you know the message was understood?

Examples of One and Two Way Communication Tools

One-Way Communication Tools	Frequency
Organization Website/Intranet	Beginning; regular updates; significant milestones
Leadership Updates - enterprise and department	Milestones and as needed
FAQs	Produced throughout, incorporated into communications and distributed during user training
Elevator Speech – Short and consistent answer to the question "what is this project?"	Develop consistent message to repeat throughout the project
Standard Project Communication Deck	Standard consistent key messages about the project that are updated at milestones and as key decisions are made
Two-Way Stakeholder Engagement Tools	**Frequency**
Meetings with Key Users and Stakeholders	Scheduled at project milestones and as clarification, understanding and agreement is required
Stakeholder Preview Sessions All Hands/Staff/Department/ Meetings in affected areas	Include on agendas in ongoing meeting. Schedule additional project-specific meetings as needed

Stakeholder Engagement Session Guidelines

Each Stakeholder Engagement session should include the following:

1. An invitation to participants that defines agenda and objectives
2. A review of agenda, objectives, and project goals at the beginning of the meeting
3. Time reserved for question and answers
4. A "Parking Lot" for documenting questions that can't be answered at the current time and follow up action items with dates for follow up

5. A plan for follow up that is explained during the presentation
6. Printed materials that restate project goals and required changes that participants can take back and share with others (as defined)
7. Multiple presenters that represent participant's areas to build credibility, leverage peer influence and make the presentation more interesting.
8. Something to "show" or "experience" to make a greater impact on participants.
9. Concrete examples or stories they can relate to that makes it "real or relevant" for them.
10. Participant Evaluation to measure presentation effectiveness and identify how to improve future sessions.

Guidelines for Defining Key Communication Messages per Phase

Phase	Questions to Answer and Key Messages to Communicate
Beginning	**Questions to Answer:** • Why are we doing this? • What is the value of this project? • Who is sponsoring this project? • Who is on the project? • How are decisions being made on this project? **Messages to Communicate** • The case for change & project vision • Link between project and achieving the organization's mission and objectives • Project team composition • Governance structure

Middle	**Questions to Answer** - Why are we doing this? - What is the benefit of the project to my area? - What have we accomplished so far? - What will be different? - When will this happen? - How will this happen? - How will I be prepared? **Messages to Communicated** - High-level overview of proposed change: what will be different - Implementation timelines and project milestones - Training Strategy - Project progress reports - Reiterate project strategic fit and vision
Pre Launch	**Questions to Answer** - How will this change how I work? - I did my job this way before. How will I do it now? - What is coming next? - Is there anything else I need to do to be ready? - How is this going to be implemented? **Messages to Communicate** - Impacts of change on all audiences - Introduction to new terms and concepts in the new environment - Action steps to prepare for implementation - Implementation strategy and schedule
Sustain – Post Go Launch	**Question to Answer** - How will I be supported in the short term and long term? **Messages to Communicate** - Support process - Results of implementation

Examples of Metrics: Communication Critical Success Factors:

You will know your communication plan is effective if the answer to each of the following statements is yes:

    a. Existing department meetings and other functional communication forums are utilized to provide regular updates, strengthen understanding and build support among stakeholders.

    b. Organizational communication is consistent in content and timely in distribution so that all employees affected by the project understand the purpose and benefits of the project, know what will be expected of them, when it will be expected and how they will be prepared.

    c. Leaders and key stakeholders in each affected area are updated on progress throughout the project and are actively involved in the communication process

    d. Leadership is highly visible and communicates effectively to support a smooth transition to new processes and systems

    e. Leaders demonstrate support for the goals of the project and the changes required to realize those goals

Key Metric:

The true "acid test" of effective communication and engagement is that anyone affected by the project can answer the following "what, why and when questions"

    1. What is the _____Project?
    2. Why are we doing this?
    3. When will it happen?
    4. What changes will we have to make to realize the benefits?
    5. What is expected of me?

Updating the Stakeholder Impact Analysis

Earlier in this chapter we reviewed the Stakeholder Impact and Influence Scale to help define the engagement objectives for key stakeholder groups. This information, along with the Impact Analysis we talked about in Chapter 2, provides valuable input to develop a broader Stakeholder Analysis Tool that helps you identify the current level and required level of stakeholder awareness, understanding, alignment, participation and ownership required for each key stakeholder group to be more effectively engaged and an integral participant in the change initiative.

As we've stated earlier, the level of support and resistance for a project will change throughout the project based on a variety of factors. The Stakeholder Analysis is a living document that is updated at key milestones throughout a project and allows you to tailor your engagement strategy to address any changes that may have occurred in a group or individual's support or resistance.

This analysis is typically done through focus groups with employees or one-on-one meetings with key stakeholders. A formal assessment tool – such as Survey Monkey – can also be used to conduct an assessment with larger stakeholder audiences.

This analysis should be done before the Stakeholder Engagement and Communication Plans are either developed or updated, based on the current phase of the project, so you can define the appropriate level of communication and engagement objectives for each stakeholder group and the most effective approach to achieve those objectives in each phase.

Using the Stakeholder Analysis to Build Change Readiness

Hans and Cynthia were successful in obtaining support from the Executive Steering Team to move forward with our plan to engage the next level of management and also secured their endorsement of the role of managers and supervisors as Change Readiness Leaders. They were also enthusiastic – for the most part – about the development of a Change Readiness Team.

Our next step was to conduct an informal Stakeholder Analysis during our meetings with managers and supervisors of the high impact areas and through focus groups with employee representatives of impacted job roles.

Engage Stakeholders Effectively

We would leverage the meetings to not only provide stakeholders with information about the project and ask for their support, but also to informally assess their current level of support or resistance, based on their current level of understanding about the project's goals and benefits, and update our engagement and communication plans accordingly.

In Chapter 2 we talked about the importance of accurately assessing impact and communicating honestly about the changes people would be required to make to those most affected. However, this alone does not guarantee readiness and may well increase resistance.

Understanding Does Not Guarantee Readiness

A group's reaction to a change effort is a combination of its **level of support** of the change effort, and its **level of understanding** of what the change effort will require. The current state of an individual or group can fall into one of the four categories listed below:

1. Support and understanding
2. Resistance and misunderstanding
3. Resistance but understanding
4. Support but misunderstanding

The relationship that may require the most work is the one characterized by support but misunderstanding. Support based on misunderstanding of the project benefits and impact will not last and will only increase mistrust for future projects. The desired goal of ownership may be achieved, but only because the individuals didn't clearly understand the true impact of the change.

Correcting misunderstandings may move the group from support to resistance, before they can experience support for the "right reasons."

If resistance is based on understanding, but not liking the benefits and/or impact, effective engagement will help you address the issues head on. It will build trust and achieve support that is lasting and for the right reasons because it is based on reality.

Bridging the Readiness Gap

The following Gap Analysis Data Collection worksheet can be used to capture the level of understanding and level of support, both current and desired, based on your impressions of the key stakeholders. This information will provide the foundation for tailoring the communication and engagement plan to bridge the gap and increase readiness.

My recommendation to Cynthia was that we use the worksheet below to record our impressions of each individual's current state of understanding, current level of support and desired level of support. This is a tool that can be reproduced for multiple groups and individuals and the results summarized on an excel spreadsheet to provide a total snapshot of the group and/or organization.

Gap Analysis Data Collection Worksheet			
Individual or Group Name	Check your estimate of the Current Level of Understanding	Check your estimate of the Current Level of Support	Check your estimate of the Desired Level of Support
	❏ Total Misunderstanding ❏ Some Misconceptions ❏ Accurate Perceptions ❏ Full Knowledge	❏ Ownership ❏ Participation ❏ Alignment ❏ Understanding ❏ Awareness ❏ Denial ❏ Complaint ❏ Opposition/Anger ❏ Sabotage ❏ Paralysis	❏ Ownership ❏ Participation ❏ Alignment ❏ Understanding ❏ Awareness

What People are saying: Helpful clues!

As we discussed in Chapter 3 on Resistance, focused listening is a very important skill to develop to hear what people are really saying. Conducting the Stakeholder Analysis provided Cynthia, and later our Change

Readiness Team members as they became more engaged in the stakeholder engagement process, an opportunity to practice this skill. I also provided them with the list below to increase their understanding of what to listen for.

Listening to what people are really saying will provide an indication of their level of resistance or support.

Here are some examples:

1. The project is our project. We are all responsible for seeing it succeed. **(Ownership)**
2. I will personally contribute to making this project a success. **(Participation)**
3. This project is a good idea. We need this to prepare us for the future **(Alignment)**
4. I understand what the project is all about. **(Understanding)**
5. I am aware that _____ is sponsoring this project and is committed to this enterprise-wide initiative. **(Awareness)**
6. What is this project all about? **(Clueless)**
7. This is just another costly program that won't make a difference. **(Complaint)**
8. The status quo is just fine. I don't agree with what the project is trying to do. **(Opposition-Anger)**
9. I like things the way they are and I'm going to find a way to keep them that way. **(Sabotage)**
10. I just don't know what to do. **(Paralysis)**

Stakeholder Map

The graph illustrated below can be used to plot the results of your analysis for each stakeholder group and provide a visual snapshot of the current level of support and understanding enterprise-wide.

It can also be used to plot the current level of support and understanding of key leaders or other individual critical stakeholders.

Are there a larger number of groups or individuals in the misunderstanding but support category?

If so, you may have enough support to implement but not the level of support you need to sustain the change.

As the illustration below shows, the goal of any change initiative is to have people **understand** the benefits and impact and **support** the project. You want to have the critical mass of stakeholder groups and key individual critical stakeholders in the understand and support quadrant.

The results of this exercise tells you where and how to invest your time to move more individuals and groups to the quadrant of understanding and support required to achieve the critical mass that allows you to both implement and sustain the change.

You are then ready to finalize your Stakeholder Engagement and Communication Plans and tailor the goals, timeline and activities needed to bring each stakeholder up to desired levels of Support. Following this approach greatly increases the effectiveness of both communication messages and engagement events and ensures that critical stakeholders have the right level of information and/or engagement at the right time to provide you with the support you need to be successful.

STAKEHOLDER MAP

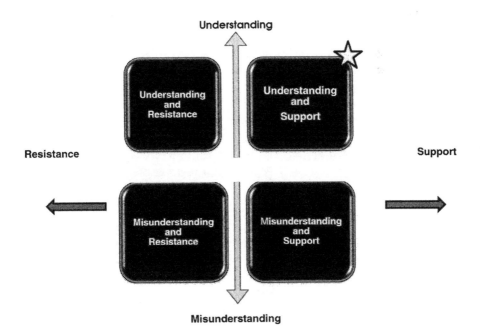

Targeting and Timing

I wanted to meet with Cynthia one more time before we presented our Stakeholder Engagement and Communication Plan recommendations to the Executive Steering Team for their endorsement. I also wanted to reemphasize the concept of "Targeting and Timing" and its application to communication and stakeholder engagement.

"Cynthia," I began," have you heard the expression that 'timing is everything'?" "Yes," she replied. "well," I continued, "that is especially true when it comes to executing communication and stakeholder engagement plans."

"I don't understand," she responded. "We have a schedule and a project plan. What timing are you talking about?"

"We all are so overwhelmed with information today that we tend to only pay attention to what is in front of us at the moment. Making sure that we have a plan that will provide the level of information people need when they need it, and only engage them when we have defined a desired outcome and prepared an agenda to achieve that outcome with that group, is critical to our success," I replied.

"Haven't we already done that," she asked?

"By assessing the level of stakeholder influence and impact, identifying key messages for different phases of the project, and choosing the most effective communication tools to convey those messages we're on the path to success," I agreed.

"The final step is to make sure the targeting and timing will provide the foundation we need to build on throughout the project to sustain or increase understanding and commitment from each group. I believe we are doing that and our plan supports that continuing. I think it will be helpful to use the model below to reconfirm that we are. We can also possibly use it as a simple way to explain to leadership why we're doing things the way we are."

"That's always helpful," she replied.

"We're following a 'cascading' approach to preparing for change that hasn't been used in this organization before. One of the reasons we're doing this is to build support through involvement but also to establish accountability at the management and executive leadership level."

The model below illustrates this cascading concept. It also reinforces that each level has a key role in engaging the next level, as we discussed in our leadership engagement discussion with Hans. We were successful in gaining his support to engage his direct reports and then with them to engage their employees and eventually to establish our Change Readiness Team in Europe."

Cascading Involvement = Expanded Ownership

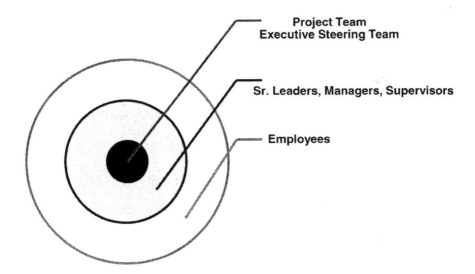

"Basically the model shows that our first target is the Executive Steering Team and Project Team. Without their understanding and support, we won't be successful in engaging the next level of the organization, senior managers, department managers and supervisors. As we engage this level we are increasing our critical mass of support across the organization. We're then better prepared to expand our engagement and communication efforts to the larger organization and to those employees most affected by the change."

"As you know, this doesn't mean that we don't communicate with employees. We communicate with the entire organization throughout the project. But, as you've seen, the content and frequency of communication and engagement is different for different stakeholder groups at different times."

Engage Stakeholders Effectively

"In the beginning, most of our time is spent with the leadership of the organization. As we move through the phases of the project the time we spend with leadership decreases and the time we spend with employees increases. We continue to engage and communicate with leadership, but on a higher and less frequent level once our plans are in place and have been endorsed".

"The execution of the change really takes place with the employees. If we follow the cascading approach, we will be better prepared to effectively communicate with and engage employees because we will have information they want to hear about what's changing and how they will be prepared for that change. They're more likely to listen to us because we have something to say that they want to hear and because we have secured the support of their management first."

"To summarize and simplify a little more," I continued, "let's call it **TADA** –

Target Audience Design Approach.

"That makes sense," Cynthia replied. "And, she continued, I can see that it's what we've really been doing all along."

"You're exactly right," I responded. "Now that we've completed the analysis phase and are finalizing our communication and engagement plans, we're ready to begin thinking about the work that will be required to prepare the organization for the change. We will continue to use the cascading approach to do this effectively. What will be different as we move into this phase is that you will see more of our work involving engaging employees and more of our communication targeted to prepare them for what will be different."

"As we engage each level, I continued, we are reemphasizing that we need them, to not only understand why we're doing this project and the changes that are required to realize the benefits, we're also asking them to **do** something to achieve and sustain success. We're letting them know that we **need** them and won't be successful without their involvement."

People feel more secure when they feel needed. Most will "rise" to the occasion if they believe their contribution will lead to a successful outcome.

"We may not get everyone on board with this concept. But, remember, we only need a critical mass."

Cascading Responsibility for Change Readiness

"So, to summarize, we're cascading involvement and ownership at all levels throughout the organization."

"We start with the Executive Steering Team and ask them to cascade to their direct reports. We work with their direct reports to prepare them to cascade to the next level of management, and then work with the next level to establish our Change Readiness Team. The Change Readiness Team cascades to employees in their areas."

"Everyone has a role. Their involvement is needed to achieve and sustain success."

"An added benefit," I continued, " is that by doing this we're not only increasing our probability of achieving a successful outcome, we're developing change readiness skills that will ultimately create a change ready organization," I concluded.

"That sounds a little beyond the scope of this project," Cynthia replied.

"I can see how you would think that," I replied, "and I can see it as and an unexpected benefit you can add to your list of accomplishments on your resume."

"Cynthia, I continued, you should be very proud of what we've accomplished over the past few weeks."

"We've regained the support we lost from some of our key stakeholders, we have a dedicated communication resource, we're building support among the managers and supervisors by cascading involvement throughout the organization and we're ready to launch our Change Readiness Team."

"We'll continue to execute and expand the scope of the Engagement and Communication Plans we've developed by beginning to focus on the work required to make sure everyone is prepared for the changes this project will bring about."

"It really is amazing when I think about it," Cynthia replied. "It's just a lot more work than I ever thought would be needed. Plus, I'm still hearing a lot of complaints."

"That's normal and will continue," I replied. "At least now you are better prepared to respond."

"We're building change readiness capability in the organization in addition to preparing for the launch of your project. What's important now is to identify what new skills, knowledge and mindset people who are affected by your project need to develop to be prepared for the changes your project will bring about."

"Are you talking about training?" Cynthia asked.

She was about to learn I meant that and more. Training alone is not enough to prepare an organization for change, as we'll discuss in the next chapter.

A Manager's Quick Guide to Achieving Change Readiness

1. Effective engagement of stakeholders is a key to success.
   a. A stakeholder is someone who has the power to influence the outcome by providing or withholding their support. A stakeholder is also anyone who will experience change in some way as a result of your project.
   b. Critical Stakeholders are individuals who have a greater degree of influence or will experience a greater change impact from your initiative. The greater the influence or impact, the more involved you want your stakeholders to be.
   c. Critical Stakeholders need to have a defined role in building change readiness. It's the action they take that provides the level of involvement they need to create an individual feeling of ownership of the outcome.
   d. Everyone has a role in making change work. The value of engaging leadership, middle managers and establishing a cross-functional Change Readiness Team cannot be underestimated. It allows you to leverage the power of peer influence to build readiness and develop change ready skills throughout the organization.
2. It's important to understand the difference between communicating and engaging,
   a. The Stakeholder Engagement Plan defines the process for effectively engaging stakeholders in a way that allows them to take ownership of the outcome rather than see themselves as "victims" of the outcome of a change initiative.
   b. The goals of engagement are to increase understanding, build alignment and create a sense of ownership of the change among people who will live with the results of the change
   c. An Engagement Plan defines how to involve key stakeholders at key points throughout the project to build change readiness.

Engage Stakeholders Effectively

d. An effective Communication Plan provides you with the structure and tools to provide accurate and consistent information on a regular basis. It helps you dispel rumors, correct misperceptions and misinformation, lessen confusion and reduce resistance throughout the project.

e. The goal of communication is to create awareness by providing accurate and timely information. The Communication Plan includes the following:
- Communication Schedule
- One and Two Way Communication Tools
- Guidelines for Defining Key Messages
- Key Metrics for Evaluating Communication Effectiveness

f. The true "acid test" of effective communication is that anyone affected by the project can answer the following "what, why and when questions:"
- What is the _____ Project?
- Why are we doing this?
- When will it happen?
- What changes will we have to make to realize the benefits?
- What is expected of me?

3. TADA is an important concept to remember. (Target Audience Design Approach)

   a. Assessing the level of stakeholder influence and impact, identifying key messages for different phases of the project, choosing the most effective communication tools to convey those messages, and following a "cascading approach" for communicating and engaging stakeholders, reinforces that each level has a key role in engaging the next level, and is needed to achieve and sustain success.

Change Readiness Thinking

Keep the following thoughts in mind to shift your thinking to a Change Readiness Mindset:

1. *If the change is significant enough to require people to learn new skills, do their work in a different way or adopt a new mindset that doesn't exist in the current culture, communication alone just isn't enough. Engaging stakeholders is the most effective method for minimizing resistance and building readiness.*

2. *We don't resist what we create. The more involved someone is in a project, the more they will feel a sense of ownership of the outcome and the greater their commitment will be to seeing it succeed.*

3. *How stakeholders are involved, as well as the role and responsibilities they are asked to take on, needs to be clearly defined and agreed to. If not, you will only create a forum for people to express opinions about what should happen, or criticize what is happening, instead of doing something themselves to achieve a successful outcome.*

4. *Everyone has a role in making change successful.*

5. *Leveraging the influence of peers is key to overcoming resistance and building support.*

6. *Managers are affected by change personally as well as being responsible for preparing their employees for change. If the manager has a change ready attitude, the employees will also. If you have the support of middle managers and supervisors, you will have the support of their employees.*

7. *Lack of information creates an opportunity for people to make up a worst case scenario about change. However, it annoys people when you inundate them with information that doesn't affect them. After a while they stop paying attention and begin ignoring the information you really want them to have.*

8. *People feel more secure when they feel needed. Most will "rise" to the occasion if they believe their contribution will lead to a successful outcome.*

CHAPTER 5:
PREPARE PEOPLE TO SUCCEED

"Will I learn what I need to know to be successful?"

We have a very short memory when it comes to preparing for change. We seem to forget about the many changes we've made in our lifetime and what we had to learn to be able to successfully make those changes.

When we're forced to learn something new our first thought is often "will I really be able to do this?"

We forget that we have been successful in learning how to do something in a different way or we wouldn't be where we are today.

We seem to forget that we have the ability to learn.

We can learn new skills. We can adapt to new working environments and differences in cultures. We can, that is, if we're provided with the tools and the training required to be successful.

The biggest mistake I've seen organizations repeatedly make is to underestimate – or sometimes even ignore - the training effort required to prepare people to perform in the new world that change creates.

So, as I was updating the Executive Steering Team on the effectiveness of our Change Readiness Strategy to date I realized that I was about to experience this phenomena again.

"We're at the point in the project where we need to do a Learning Needs Analysis to estimate the training effort required for this project to be successful, I began."

Prepare People to Succeed

"Training effort?" Stan, the director of sales and marketing, interrupted. "What training? "Our employees don't have time to go to training. They need to be out in the field selling and making money. They're smart. They'll figure out on their own what they need to know. Plus, this project is costing enough already. You're not telling me we're going to have to spend even more money on training, are you?"

"That's exactly what I'm telling you," I replied. "You're going to pay for training whether you do it formally or not."

"If you don't take the time to train people before you go-live with the change, you'll pay for it in lower productivity from the time they'll spend learning it on their own. You'll pay for it with the longer time it will take you to realize ROI because people weren't adequately prepared to perform in a way that would allow you to realize benefits sooner."

"Not to mention, the increased lack of trust in leadership employees will feel because we've spent all this time talking about preparing for change with our change readiness efforts and then do nothing to actually equip them with the skills they need to be able to perform successfully. The price tag on a lack of trust is pretty high and will cost you on this project as well as ones you launch in the future."

"Rita is correct," Hans replied. "It makes no sense to continue with this project if we aren't going to provide people with the training they need to be successful."

"I agree with Stan," Charles chimed in. "We don't have the budget and our employees don't have the time. Can't we just send them something to read?"

"That sounds like a good solution to me," Bill agreed.

I was relying on peer pressure to win this battle for me so I allowed the discussion to continue hoping more of the others would speak up and agree with Hans. Jo Anne, the director from Cape Town, finally did.

"I just want to remind you all," she began, "that this is the 3rd time we've attempted this project. We've agreed so far to do things differently this time. We want to learn from, and not repeat, mistakes from the past. Until now, I think we've done quite well. I can't believe that we would get to this point in the project and be willing to risk failure because we don't want to spend the time or money to train people for the changes we've decided are needed. That just doesn't make good business sense to me," she concluded quite emphatically.

"It doesn't make sense to me either, and it's not the approach we're going to take on this project, "Dennis, the CIO declared.

This was somewhat shocking to everyone since Dennis rarely attended the Executive Steering Team meetings and seldom spoke up when he did.

"Rita," Cynthia spoke up, "you've made recommendations before that we rejected because we've never really prepared for change well in the past and didn't understand what we needed to do and why or how we needed to do it. This whole change readiness process has been a change for us. I've learned a lot and I'm still learning."

"Why don't you explain the approach you recommend, in a little more detail, and give us time to understand what is required?. We'll then be in a better position to make a decision at our next meeting. I think everyone here can agree to that," she confidently stated.

Cynthia had come a long way since our first meeting.

"Thanks for the suggestion Cynthia," Dennis responded. I'm sure there's no one here who disagrees with that. We'll look forward to getting more information from Rita and making a decision on 'how' - not 'if' - we'll make sure our people have the skills and knowledge they need for this project to be successful and for our organization to realize the ROI we expect."

The silence was deafening.

I finally spoke up and said "I'll have my recommended approach outlined, including learning options, and send to each of you by the end of the week. Thank you all for supporting this next step."

The reality was that not everyone supported the next step, I just needed to think that they did.

The Difference between Training and Learning

Often when people hear "training," the thought that enters their mind is about being bored sitting in a classroom all day, reviewing a much too large manual and listening to information that has little to do with their day-to-day job.

> *Effective learning is not accomplished in a "one-size-fits-all" type of training.*

Effective training is designed to teach individuals what they need to know, and be able to do, to perform **their** work once the change is implemented.

Prepare People to Succeed

Classroom instruction may not be the best training method, and it definitely shouldn't be the only method used to equip people with the knowledge and skills required to do their job.

When we identify what people need to **learn,** we can also choose the most effective method for delivering that information. This is the benefit of conducting a Learning Needs Analysis.

This was the first step I discussed with Cynthia when I reviewed the Learning Project Plan illustrated below. This is the plan we would present to the Executive Steering Team so they would understand that we needed to follow a structured approach, to identify learning needs of everyone affected by the project, and have the information required to develop an effective Learning Program.

Once we achieved their understanding and support for this approach, we would review it with our Change Readiness Network. Since one of their key responsibilities is ensuring that people in their area are prepared for change, it was important for us to obtain their understanding and support for our approach. It was also critical for them to know this was an approach their leadership supported.

Learning Project Plan

PHASE	ACTIVITIES
Assess And Plan	• Agree on learning expectations, objectives and approach • Agree on learning materials and timeline for completion • Establish Learning Team to oversee execution of the Learning Plan • Agree on roles and responsibilities • Identify learning audiences • Assess learning needs • Analyze results and finalize recommendations for delivery methods
Design and Develop	• Identify courses based on learning needs and delivery methods • Design role-based curriculum • Develop course materials, exercises, job aids • Conduct SME review of materials • Approve course materials • Finalize materials for train-the-trainer and one-on-one on the job coaching

Prepare Delivery	• Conduct Train-the-Trainer sessions • Create training schedule and plan training logistics • Identify instructors per session • Prepare instructors • Conduct pilot sessions • Revise learning materials based on outcome of pilot session
Deliver "Just in Time"	• Deliver employee learning sessions • Evaluate effectiveness • Develop additional job aids based on FAQs and session feedback • Designate "go-to" mentors for employees after launch
Provide Post Launch Employee Support	• Identify appropriate follow-up activities • Implement follow-up activities • Implement post-launch support

I reviewed the plan with Cynthia and explained that, by adding start and end dates to each phase of the Learning Plan, we could use this same document as a checklist to make sure we were on target with the timeline required for the organization to be ready for implementation.

There were a few more tools and templates I needed to review with Cynthia so she would understand the additional work required to finalize a training plan. This included a

1. Learning Needs Assessment
2. Skill Profile
3. Learning Delivery Options
4. Learning Strategy.

We would not present all of these tools to Executive Steering Team, although we would to the Change Readiness Team since they would be participating in our Learning Needs Analysis.

We would be providing training for the member of the Change Readiness Team to prepare them to use the tools to do the assessment work themselves for their own organization. This is one application of the cascading of change ownership strategy we talked about in the previous chapter on involvement.

Learning Needs Assessment

I explained to Cynthia that there are many methods and tools we could use to conduct a Learning Needs Assessment. What's important is that the assessment be designed to effectively gather information on the following:

1. **Who is the learning audience?**
   a. Who will need to have new knowledge, skills or be required to think or behave differently for the change to be successful?
   b. How large is this group? Where are they located?
2. **What new knowledge is required? What will employees need to know or do for the change to be successful?**
   a. Skills
   b. Behavior
   c. Process or System
   d. Policy or regulations
3. **What is the depth of learning required by each group?**
   a. What level of knowledge is required to perform effectively?
   b. Do they need to be an expert, do they need to be able to teach others or do they only need a level of awareness?
   c. How often will they use the new skill or knowledge? Every day? Rarely?
4. **What is the preferred learning method?**
   a. How have they learned most effectively in the past? Self-study, on the job training, mentoring, classroom instruction, CBTs etc.?
   b. Is "hands-on" instruction required for employees to achieve the level of expertise or to prepare for the frequency of use?

"Sounds pretty simple," Cynthia responded. That was before she saw what a Learning Needs Analysis looked like.

I introduced the template by saying, "now Cynthia, you have to keep in mind that this is an example of a Learning Needs Analysis that is scalable to fit our needs. We may or may not need one this comprehensive. Or, we may need to do one this detailed for Europe, since they are experiencing the greatest change and will need to learn the most, but definitely not for Canada or some of the marketing and sales job roles."

"That's good," she responded, "since Bill wasn't exactly supportive of the whole idea of training and the time his people would need to take away from the field to attend training sessions."

Example of a Learning Needs Assessment

"The first step we need to take," I explained, "is to scope out the level of training effort we think will be required. We don't have all the details yet. We do know enough to estimate how complex or simple the training program will be, so we can provide leadership with the information they need to approve the resources and budget that will be required to prepare the organization."

"The Learning Scope Analysis illustrated below can be used to estimate the level of training required to equip employees with the knowledge and skills needed to continue to perform their job successfully after the change is implemented. "

"It is scalable to the size of the learning audience and can be reproduced on an Excel spreadsheet to enable tailoring and sorting by job role, type of knowledge needed, and level of learning effort required. We can add as many columns as we need to evaluate each new skill employees will need to learn and rows for the number of job roles who will need to learn something new or change the way they currently work."

"By using a numeric scale, we can estimate the overall level of training effort required by department, job role and the entire organization for the project to be successful. The higher the overall score by role, department, knowledge type, etc., the larger the training effort."

"After we have this information," I continued, "we will want to do a Skill Profile for each critical role – which would be the roles with the highest scores - so that we can decide on the most effective method for learning content development and delivery."

"It may sound a little complicated," I said in response to the look on Cynthia's face, "but we'll take it one step at a time. As we gather and compile the information into an overall plan, it will begin to make sense and you'll be glad we took this approach."

"Having this information provides the basis for developing a Learning Plan that is tailored to meet the needs of the employees instead of taking a "one-size-fits-all" approach to training that isn't effective and would probably be more expensive in the long run."

"Remember," I reemphasized, "we're learning from past mistakes and changing the way we do things on this project. Following a more formal process to identifying learning needs and tailoring training to meet those needs, is one of the changes we're recommending."

Learning Scope Analysis

Scoping Criteria:	Scale
C = Complexity of Activity	**Complexity Criteria:**
	0 = not performed
	1 = Slight change from today
	2 = New task
	3 = New technology and new process
	4 = Complex technology and processes
F = Frequency of Use	**Frequency Criteria:**
	0 = not performed
	1 = limited use/activity
	2 = moderate use/activity
	3 = daily use/activity
L = Level of Knowledge Required	**Summary Criteria Numbers:**
	1 = "Knowledge"
	2 = "Comprehension"
	3 = "Hands on"
	4 = Expert

Q = Number of Users	End User Quantity Criteria:
	0 = none
	1 = 10 - 50
	2 = 50 - 200
	3 = Over 200
	4 = Over 200 in multiple locations

Example of Application:

The example below illustrates how the information gathered from the above analysis can be categorized by skill level for different job roles. Using an Excel spreadsheet to document the information makes it easier to "slice and dice" the results in multiple ways. This can include knowledge required by each job role as well as overall effort required by each department or enterprise-wide. It also provides the first step in developing a role-based curriculum.

JOB ROLE ANALYSIS

Job Role	Skill				Skill				Total
	C	F	L	Q	C	F	L	Q	
Engineer	4	3	3	3	2	3	3	3	24
Marketing Rep	3	1	1	2	2	1	1	2	13
HR Analyst	3	3	3	0	4	4	3	0	19
Accounting Clerk	3	3	3	3	4	3	3	3	25
Data Entry	3	3	3	3	2	1	1	3	19
Customer service Rep	3	2	2	3	2	3	3	3	21

(Skill example: follow new process, use new technology, learn new compliance requirement)

Interpretation

"Looking at the example above, we can conclude that the overall training effort for Engineers and Accounting Clerks will be greater. But, we can't assume that because the score for HR Analyst was lower their training will be easy. If we look at the score for complexity, frequency and level of knowledge, their score is high. It's a lower overall score because there aren't as many people in that job role. The audience is smaller but the knowledge needed is just as complex as that of the engineer."

"The complexity score can also tell us which skill will require the most in depth and hands-on training. We can use this information to determine how we develop the training content and choose the most effective method for instruction."

"We also need to look at the frequency. The complexity score is high for certain skills for Marketing Reps, but since they don't use that skill very often we can use a different training approach for them. This could be possibly identifying a mentor they can call or producing a job aid they will have available to guide them through the steps when they do use that skill. It wouldn't make sense to put them through intensive training when it may be a long time before they ever perform that task. But, that's part of the next analysis we'll do."

"I can see how this tool could be used by each manager to understand the training needs of her department," Cynthia responded.

"Yes," I replied, "it's a very scalable and adaptable tool. Our approach would be to work with each member of the Change Readiness Team to conduct the Learning Needs Assessment in his/her area. A key part of their role is to keep their management informed as well."

"At the same time, we want to understand the involvement your corporate training group needs so that they will be able to support the ongoing learning effort company-wide after the change has been implemented.

> *We have to think long term as well as short term.*
> *What do we need to do now for us to have a successful implementation*
> *and what is required long term to sustain the benefits?*

"The assessment results for each area will be combined to create the enterprise-wide assessment that helps us understand the size and scope of the overall training effort as well as the individual needs of each department. That will provide us with the information we need to select the most effective method – both from a learning and cost perspective - to develop and deliver training."

"So, if I understand correctly," Cynthia replied, "the Learning Needs Assessment provides us with the big picture of learning needs for job roles, the department and overall organization to understanding the size and scope of the training effort."

"The Skill Profile provides us with a more targeted picture of the knowledge needs of the critical roles – those experiencing the greatest amount of change – and what they will need to know to be prepared to successfully do their job after the change is implemented."

"Both of these tools provide information that helps us choose the most effective method to use to develop and deliver training."

"You've got it right," I replied. "I just wanted to add," I continued, "that because adults learn best by doing, any training approach we use will include some type of 'hands-on' activities."

"Now, let's take a closer look at the Skill Profile Model and discuss the various learning methods. Then you'll understand the basis for the high-level training approach we'll present to the Executive Steering Team, and be able to help me explain all of this in more detail to prepare our Change Readiness Team to use the tools."

Skill Profile

As I mentioned earlier, once the larger, more comprehensive Learning Assessment is completed, it's beneficial to develop Skill Profiles for the critical roles that will experience the greatest degree of change or whose performance is critical to sustaining the change.

The information from the Skill Profile can also be used to develop a role based curriculum to guide the development of a more effective tailored learning approach.

The Skill Profile Model can be applied to a job role to determine what learning needs will be required for a specific critical role across the organization, or used to create a high-level picture of the requirements for a department or the entire organization.

Before using the model, it's important to define what we mean when we use the term "skill."

What is a "skill?"

A skill describes the knowledge and ability you have to perform tasks. Skills can also include personal traits that are elements of your personality that make you more effective in performing certain job roles.

Some people find it easier to think about skills as nouns, verbs, and adjectives.

Nouns answer the question: "What knowledge do I need to have that I don't have now to be able to do my job once the change takes place?"

Verbs answer the question: "What do I need to be able to 'do' that I don't have the ability to do now?"

Adjectives are more descriptive of the culture that needs to exist to support the performance required for success. Adjectives answer the question of "How do I need to think or behave in order for the change to be successful?"

Identifying how a culture needs to change and what to do to bring a change in behavior about however, is often overlooked.

Culture describes the behaviors people believe are required to fit in and meet expectations within their organization. In its simplest terms it has been defined as "the way things get done around here."

What is the new mindset? What are the new behaviors? What adjectives describe the culture required for success currently and in the future?

Once you have this information, you can assess the gap between the current culture and the one required in the future and begin to identify what the solution is for bridging this gap.

The solution may consist of some combination of training, coaching, new performance rewards, leadership reinforcements, updating of the corporate mission and vision or other changes in the working environment.

Although changing a culture is a long term project, it is important to understand that there are changes in culture that will be required for the goals of any organizational change to be realized. Training alone is not enough. We'll discuss more about culture change in the Chapter 7 on Sustaining Change.

The Skill Profile Model shown below illustrates how the three elements of a skill fit together to create a snapshot of an individual's current skills and/or to create a profile of the new skills that will be required. The gap between the current sill profile and future skill requirements defines the learning requirements for each job role.

SKILL PROFILE	
Nouns = Knowledge	**What will I need to KNOW that I don't know now?**
Verbs = Actions	**What will I need to be able to DO that I don't do now?**
Adjectives = Attitude/Behavior	**How do I need to think or behave that is different from how I think and behave today?**

The Learning Needs Assessment and Skill Profile are tools that allow you to define the knowledge and behaviors required for the change to be sustained. You can then establish realistic expectations with leadership about the effort that will be required and help them understand that it takes more than training on a new system or process to adequately prepare an organization for change

These tools also provide valuable information to develop the Organizational Readiness Plan that we will discuss in more depth in the next chapter.

Learning Delivery Methods

After we have identified what people need to know, do and think to be prepared to work in a different way once the change is implemented, we have a better understanding about what the content of the training should cover.

The next step is to decide on the most effective method for delivering this information to people so that they can understand and apply it in their day-to-day world.

Although individuals have different styles of learning, we all learn best by doing. Based on my experience, the following methods have proven to be the most effective for adult learners:

1. **Role-Based**
   - Training content and activities are tailored to how employees will perform their current job once the change takes place. This makes it more "real" for them.

2. **Train-the-trainer /Mentor**
   - Employees are chosen to serve as SMEs to assist with developing training content, deliver training to their peers and serve as mentors who answer questions and provide support after the change is implemented.
   - Employees are chosen for this role based on their credibility with peers, knowledge of existing business operations, processes and any new technology that is being implemented.
   - External training experts provide training for employees who will serve as trainers and mentors.`

3. **A Blended combination of learning methods that can include:**
   - Instructor-led classroom training
   - On-line documentation
   - Simulations/CBT
   - One-on-one sessions

Selection of Learning Method

The table below lists various learning methods and criteria for choosing each option or a combination of options you think will be most effective in your organization.

LEARNING METHODS	
On the Job (OJT)	**Description:** • Mentor or other "coach" walks trainee through an outline of job tasks • Provides structured, supervised practice opportunities • Monitors proficiency • Usually occurs in the workplace **Recommended when:** • Training audience is small • Skills are complex; extensive feedback and practice is required • People are available to serve as mentors/coaches
Instructor Presentation	**Description:** • Expert instructor delivers activity-based and scripted training, provides feedback and learning evaluation **Recommended when:** • Audience is medium to large • Materials have a medium to long shelf-life • Participant discussion is required • Supervised practice is required • Adequate training facilities are available and/or obtainable • Enough experts are available to deliver the course to all audiences within the allotted time
Classroom Instruction Followed by Coaching	**Description:** • This can be combined with expert instructor-led classroom training. • Expert instructor delivers activity-based, scripted training and learning evaluations • Coaches/Mentors provide reinforcement of training and just-in-time help • Opportunities are provided for immediate application of learning back on the job, with a coach to provide guidance if needed **Recommended when:** • Audience is small or a large number of mentors are available to support small groups • Materials have a short to medium shelf-life • Participant discussion is required • Supervised practice is required • An expert mentor or coach is available to provide post-classroom support within the allotted time

Learning Networks **Problem Solving Teams**	**Description:** • Teams are established to support or reinforce learning. We learn best when we have to explain concepts and procedures to others. • Encourage formulation of "learning networks," learners who attended training together and can call on each other with questions/problems after they are back on the job • Establish problem solving teams to identify and discuss problems. • Ask newly trained employees to train others. **Recommended when:** • Cross-functional interaction is beneficial • Continuous improvement is a goal • Processes are being standardized across functions • Someone is available to lead or facilitate networks or team so they don't dissolve into complaint sessions • "Back-ups" for the experts to strengthen internal knowledge is desired
Self-Study	**Description:** • Trainees are given materials to study at their own pace, usually written materials, activities, or on-line tutorials **Recommended when:** • Audience is medium to large • Materials have a medium to long shelf-life • An expert supervisor or coach is available to monitor progress and proficiency • Mastery is less critical
Computer-Based Training (CBT)	**Description:** • Job tasks are closely simulated on-line; materials are presented via text, graphics, audio, or video; performance feedback is provided on-line **Recommended when:** • Audience is large (>200) and distributed • Materials have a long shelf-life (>2 years) • Mastery is critical • Delivery technology is available and/or obtainable • Recurring need for training

Demos or Preview Sessions **Big-Picture Brown-Bags**	**Description:** • Some learners need to relate their jobs/skills to an overall concept. • Provide a high-level demonstration of how technology will be used or an overview of a new process. • Schedule occasional brown-bag lunches or workshops that educate employees on the "big-picture" and help them understand how their successful performance relates to overall business goals. **Recommended when:** • Leaders don't need to attend training but do need to a high-level overview of what will be different for employees • There is confusion or mis-communication about the purpose and benefits of the project • A training pre-requisite or reinforcement of a key change or new functionality is needed • An expert is available to lead the session
Communication	**Description:** • Information is provided through email or bulletins that employees may review at individual pace. **Recommended when:** • Audience is large (>200) and distributed • Materials have a long shelf-life (>2 years) • Mastery is less critical • Recurring need to train
Desk References	**Description:** • Provide curriculum/references that can be used to reinforce key points for just-in-time training. **Recommended when:** • Skill isn't used or knowledge isn't needed on a regular basis • Materials have a long shelf life • Reinforcement or reminders of key changes need to be easily available

Prepare People to Succeed

Job Aid	Description:
	• High-level summary or illustration of key steps required to access and use system and/or follow a key process
	Recommended when:
	• Reinforcement of key process is critical
	• System usage is infrequent so a "quick-tip" reminder of what to do to use system is more effective
	• Information is job-role specific
	• Information can be summarized and/or illustrated effectively in a small amount of space

Learning Strategy: Pulling it all Together

After reviewing the learning tools and agreeing on the approach we felt would be most effective in preparing employees to succeed in the new world, we were ready to finalize our Learning Strategy and present our recommendations to the Executive Steering Team.

The Learning Strategy would include the following:

1. Learning Project Plan with dates, roles and responsibilities for each phase.
2. An example of the Learning Needs Assessment
3. An overview of how the Learning Needs Assessment would be executed by the Change Readiness Team members in each area and the results combined into a comprehensive Learning Plan for the organization
4. An example of a Learning Plan that would list the courses that would be offered and the individuals who would be required to attend those courses.

Meeting with Leadership

The agenda we put together for the Executive Steering Team Meeting, and an example that could guide you in seeking approval from your leadership, included the following:

1. Learning Strategy Objectives and Critical Success Factors
2. Learning Project Phases, Timeline and Activities
3. Overview of Recommended Learning Strategy and Analysis Tools
    a. Scope of Training to Prepare for Go-Live
    b. Scope of Training to Sustain Knowledge in the Organization
4. Learning Development and Delivery Roles and Responsibilities
    a. Develop
    b. Deliver
    c. Coordinate
    d. Sustain
5. Training Content Approval Process
6. Learning Curriculum and Schedule Development Process
7. Mentor Role and Recommendations for Post Go Live Support

Right in the middle of the presentation Stan interrupted to say, "I have to admit that I was somewhat skeptical of the need to invest a lot of time and money into training. I just didn't see that this was something we needed to do. I started thinking differently after our National Sales and Marketing Meeting last week".

"These guys are really nervous about the changes this project will bring about. They've been doing things the same way for so long. We haven't kept up with the changing times so our guys aren't very 'tech savvy'. They really are concerned about learning new technology and adapting to new processes. The last thing we want is for our sales people to feel less confident in their ability to be successful in their job. On top of that, he continued, they have little confidence in our ability to successfully pull this project off - after all, this is our 3rd attempt – and no faith that leadership will provide them with the training they need to be successful."

"Well," Bill interrupted, "I'll agree that we don't exactly have a good track record when it comes to training. It's either sink or swim. Our approach has been that they'll learn as they go along and figure it out on their own."

"That's worked ok in the past," Stan continued, "but I don't think it will work now. I support the approach Rita is recommending and anything else we can do to increase our employees' confidence in their ability to learn what they'll need to know to continue to be successful in their job after this change is implemented."

Understanding the influence and power of peer pressure that had just taken place, I knew there was little more I needed to say.

"It sounds like we have agreement to move forward with engaging the Change Readiness Team in conducting our Learning Needs Analysis," I began, "I will provide each one of you with the information you need to communicate with your direct reports about how this will take place and to reemphasize your full support of this process."

"We'll have follow up discussions with your managers so they understand the timeline for engaging their area and also when and how they will be provided with the results of the analysis."

"Remember that continuing to follow the "cascading" approach we're using as an involvement model for this project is key to our success."

"As Stan and Bill pointed out, we want to make sure that each employee who is affected by this project has the trust and confidence that their leadership will do what it takes to ensure that they are prepared with the skills and knowledge they need to continue to be successful in doing their job. It's important that each one of you - and each one of your managers - reinforce that as often as possible."

"Also, involving the Change Readiness Team in conducting the analysis, providing input into the final approach, and using them as SMEs and mentors, will reinforce that leadership is committed to this project's success."

"There's one other thought I want to leave you with," I concluded. "Training is only one component of what it takes to prepare an organization for change. Although it's a very important one, there are other key activities that will become part of our overall Readiness Plan.

We'll talk more about that over the next few weeks."

Preparing the Change Readiness Team

After obtaining approval from leadership to move forward with our Learning Strategy, the next step was to launch the Change Readiness Team and prepare them to do the job we were asking them to do.

The cascading approach described earlier had work very well. By working with the middle management level, we had been able to assemble a cross-functional team of individuals who represented the job roles and functional areas that would experience the greatest change impact from our project.

In our discussions with middle management, we emphasized the power of peer influence and the importance of selecting someone for the Change Readiness Team that had credibility and was respected by his/her peers.

We prepared a Change Readiness Team Orientation session that would provide each team member with the following:

1. An overview of the project goals, benefits and timeline
2. The results of the Impact Analysis described in Chapter Two that describe the changes that would be required to realize those benefits
3. A high-level overview of our Change Readiness Plan that included our Stakeholder Analysis, Communication and Engagement Plan and Learning Strategy. We emphasized that although we would be following the same approach, the tools and templates we would be using could be tailored to address issues unique to each area
4. A description of the role and responsibilities of the Change Readiness Team members in executing the Change Readiness Plan and my role as an external consultant in preparing and coaching them through the process of doing what we were asking them to do.
5. Critical success factors for the team that answered the question: "we will know we have been successful in our role as Change Liaisons if the following happens........." The Critical Success Factors became our guidelines for making decisions as a team. They were items we could refer back to and ask "will taking this action or making this decision achieve one or more of our Critical Success Factors? If not, why would we do it?"

We invited the members of the Executive Steering Team to attend the beginning hour of the orientation to show their support for the project, reinforce the importance of the Change Readiness Team, communicate their trust in the ability of the individuals of the team to perform their role in preparing their area for change.

> *Visible and vocal leadership support is essential for a*
> *Change Readiness Team to be successful*

Following the orientation, the team agreed to attend two half-day training sessions to learn the basic principles of change readiness, techniques for refocusing resistance and how to use the tools and templates we had agreed on. The team would then meet for one hour weekly to receive project updates and provide updates on progress being made in their area and to escalate any issues they were identifying that could prevent a successful implementation in their area.

At the end of the two half-day training sessions, I felt that I had developed enough trust with the members of the Change Readiness Team to have an open and honest conversation about what people *really* thought about the project and what would be the biggest obstacles we would have to overcome to achieve a successful rollout and sustain the benefits.

Their response was honest, direct and quite shocking to Cynthia, who I had invited to attend.

I had planned a debrief with Cynthia after the session ended. Before I could say anything she blurted out "there is no way this project will ever be successful! Did you hear what they said? They don't even support it completely."

"Cynthia, what they said provided us with an accurate snapshot of the organization's current perception of the project. It's information. It's not a prediction. We can use this information to tailor our Change Readiness Plans to address the real issues, current misconceptions, and understand what it will take to prepare the organization for a successful launch. "If you remember," I continued, "we went through the same experience with the Executive Steering Team after our initial Impact Analysis. We survived that and strengthened our support and we'll survive this and strengthen our support with the Change Readiness Team."

"I know, I know what you're going to say," she interrupted, "we don't need 100% we just need a critical mass to be ready."

"That's right," I responded. "We're not ready for go-live now, but we don't need to be. We just need to be ready to take the next step."

"What's that?" she asked.

"It's developing our Readiness Assessment that we will use with the team to track where we are and where we need to be to be ready to go-live. It will be the basis for our go/no go decision from an organizational readiness perspective"

"We'll establish readiness criteria and use a red, yellow, and green color coding system to provide a readiness snapshot on a monthly, bi-monthly and then weekly basis as we get closer to our go-live date."

"At this point," she said, "it's probably all red."

"Maybe. Maybe not." I replied.

"I know. I know, " she said. "We don't need it to be all green."

"Not at the moment," I responded. "But, we will before we go live. Let's get together tomorrow so I can review an example with you that we'll introduce to leadership and our Change Readiness Team in a few weeks."

A Manager's Quick Guide to Achieving Change Readiness

1. People often resist change because they lack confidence in their ability to learn something new or "fit" in a new culture change creates.
    a. *They need reassurance that they will be provided with training before change is implemented and support after change is implemented that will prepare them to continue to perform successfully*
2. Change requires people to learn new skills and often to develop a new mindset
    a. *A skill is the knowledge and ability required to complete a task*
    b. *Personal characteristics are also skills that can be strengths in the current culture or become liabilities in a different culture.*
    c. *People need to be prepared for the impact of culture change and new behavior or mindset changes required to perform successfully*
3. Training that is delivered as a "one-size-fits-all" classroom instruction can overwhelm people with information but not provide them with the knowledge they need to do their job in a different way.
    a. *A Learning Needs Assessment and Skill Profile should be completed to identify role-based learning needs and assess the level of complexity so that the most effective method for instruction or mentoring can be chosen*
4. Adequately preparing an organization for change involves more than training
    a. *Additional "readiness" factors will be discussed in the next chapter*

Change Readiness Thinking

Keep the following thoughts in mind to shift your thinking to a Change Readiness Mindset:

1. The longer we do a job in the same way, the more likely we are to forget that we have the ability to learn how to do things in a new way.

2. Learning something new is like learning to write with your left hand if you are right handed or with your right if you are left handed. It will slow you down and feel uncomfortable until you get use to the new way. Productivity in an organization is affected in the same way when people are learning a new way of working.

3. Adequately assessing learning needs, choosing the most effective form of preparation, and providing mentoring before and after the change can minimize the impact on productivity.

4. Spending millions of dollars on new technology and not enough on preparing people to use the new technology or thinking they will be able to figure it out on their own, is just plain stupid.

5. If you decide to establish a change network or use mentors or super users for a train-the-trainer, make sure they have the knowledge and leadership support they need to be successful.

6. Leadership support of training is critical. Encourage leaders to require people – especially those roles critical to the success of your project – to attend training.

CHAPTER 6:
EVALUATE READINESS FOR LAUNCH

"Are we really going to do this?"

As the deadline for going live comes closer, there is a mix of anticipation, reticence and disbelief. I start hearing comments such as:

"After three attempts are we finally going to do this?"

"Are we really ready for this?"

Even, "are we sure this is what we want to do? Maybe we should take a step back and rethink this. It's not too late to change our mind."

We were sliding up and down on the Readiness Scale. One day we were optimistic that all indicators pointed to a successful go-live and the next day we were sure that disaster loomed ahead.

We had done a great job of talking about the future and developing and redeveloping the project plan that would make the future a reality. Now we were at the go-no-go point of no return.

Talking about change is one thing. Actually doing it is something else entirely.

Especially when you've made previous attempts that haven't been successful.

"Are we ready?" is an appropriate question to ask. That question can only be answered with accuracy and confidence if the meaning of "being ready" has been defined, discussed and agreed to by the people responsible for making the decision to implement the change.

Key Questions to Determine Readiness

At this point in a project, leadership should be able to answer the following questions:

1. **What does "being ready" mean we are "ready" to do?** Does it mean that we are *ready* to:
    a. Implement the change?
    b. Sustain the change?
    c. Implement the change everywhere at the same time?
    d. Implement the change in a phased approach that could consist of implementing some of the changes now and some later or rolling out the change to different areas at different times?
2. ***How* do we know we are ready?**
    a. What criteria are we using to evaluate our level of readiness?
3. ***Who* decides that we are ready?**
    a. Who evaluates the level of readiness to provide input into that decision?
4. **What do we *do* if we're *not ready*?**
    a. Do we have a "Plan B?"

One could argue that these are questions that should have been answered before a decision was made to undertake a project. My experience has been that this doesn't happen.

Organizations typically don't take the time to evaluate change impact and the change capability of the organization and those affected before undertaking a project that will require enterprise-wide change.

There would probably be a higher success rate if leadership did take the time to understand the organizational impact of any decision they are about to make, take into consideration other initiatives occurring at the same time, and/or affecting the same employees, that could tip the scales into the danger zone of one too many changes for employees to handle and greatly increase the probability of another "failed" project.

If your project is the "typical" project where this wasn't done in the beginning, you can use the following information to evaluate the level of readiness before going live. This will provide you with the evaluation criteria you need, from an organizational perspective, to incorporate into the process of making a "go/no go" decision.

Organizational Readiness Plan

The answers to the four questions that follow provide the basic structure for the Organizational Readiness Plan. Let's look at each of these questions in more depth.

1. **WHAT DOES 'BEING READY' MEAN WE ARE READY TO DO?**

    Basically, there are three ways to implement change:
    1. Big Bang – everybody everywhere at the same time
    2. Phased – staggered roll out to different areas or roles at different times
    3. Pilot – rollout to a small "test" group and evaluate results before rolling out to the larger organization

Ideally, the decision on how to rollout the change would have been made once the Organizational Impact Analysis we discussed in Chapter Two is completed.

The Impact Analysis and expanded Stakeholder Analysis described in Chapter Four, provides an opportunity to assess the ability of different areas to absorb the change based on certain factors such as leadership support, degree of change, potential impact to day-to-day operations and past history of managing change.

This information is a good indicator of where in the organization there is a higher probability of success and a lower probability of failure.

If an organization's history of change is not good, and the degree of impact is high, a phased or pilot approach rather than a "big-bang" is a better choice.

Another reason that this decision should be made earlier in the project is that it affects the Learning Strategy Plan we discussed in the previous chapter. The probability of success is increased if people are trained as close to implementation as possible.

The Learning Strategy should support the timeline for implementation –whether phased, pilot or big bang.

Pros and Cons of Implementation Options

There are pros and cons of each of the three options described above that need to be evaluated before a decision is made.

A phased approach extends the project timeline and will probably increase the cost. It can, however, lessen the overall impact to the organization and provide an opportunity to "test" the change or rollout approach with a smaller group and make adjustments before rolling out to a larger group. If the rollout is successful, the "first-group-out" becomes the model for success and stronger advocates. You can leverage this peer influence in rolling out to the larger organization. Of course the reverse can happen if the rollout doesn't go well.

A big-bang approach communicates that the organization is serious about this change. Not doing it – or only partially doing it – is not an option.

Often, this decision is based purely on budget and not on an evaluation of the readiness of the organization. That's why the probability of failure is higher with a "big-bang" than with a phased approach. This approach is high risk, requires broader and more in-depth preparation and is being done less often.

Having a robust Readiness Plan becomes even more important when the big bang approach to implementation is chosen.

Another important factor in this decision, that organizations often overlook, is how prepared the organization is to sustain the change.

If the project team members are the only ones who have been driving the project, and the employees who are going to be the ones to sustain the change haven't been involved along the way, they aren't going to be ready to assume responsibility for sustaining the changes that have been implemented when the project ends and the team is disbanded.

To avoid this happening, the "owners" of maintaining the change – or operationalizing the change so it becomes the new normal way business is done – must be identified early on and a plan developed for transitioning ownership from project team members to these individuals.

If the change is a process change, this can be achieved by naming process owners who are recognized as process experts and are responsible for monitoring the effectiveness, enforcing compliance, and making recommendations for continuous improvements.

If the change is a technology change, mentors or "super users" can be designated and involved in the preparation phase of the project. They receive more in-depth training, participate in the train-the-trainer program and are ready to take on this expert role to provide support at go-live and serve as the official "go-to" person for assistance after go live.

For any type of change, establishing a Change Leadership Team and/or Change Readiness Network early in the project creates a structure where process owners, mentors or designated SPOCs (Single Points of Contact) provide a link between the project team and the organization. This makes the transition from a project to ongoing operations much smoother, greatly increases readiness for change and the probability that benefits the project was created to achieve will actually be realized.

Being ready to "go-live" with a project means being ready and able to "sustain" the activities that will allow the organization to realize the benefits the project was expected to deliver

2. HOW DO WE KNOW WE ARE READY?

I have learned that decision making at critical milestones of a project is easier if people have established concrete indicators that tell them they are on the right track and that they are making the right decision. The best approach to evaluating readiness is to do it along the way.

Most organizations follow a phased project management approach with a "decision gate" at the end of each phase. Certain criteria must be met to move forward to the next phase of the project. If those criteria haven't been met, the project can be put on hold until it is met and they are ready to move to the next phase.

Including readiness indicators in the decision criteria for moving from one phase to the next provides an opportunity to identify and address organizational issues along the way and not allow them to become obstacles to a successful launch when it's time to implement.

> *Having a Readiness Checklist provides documentation for individuals who are responsible for making the go-no-go decision and a higher level of confidence that they are making the right decision.*

This Readiness Checklist is tailored to evaluate what needs to exist from an organizational/people perspective at each phase of the project and what needs to be in place to make the decision at the final phase that the organization is ready to implement. It would include the categories illustrated in the example below with criteria to evaluate the current state of each category.

Although the criteria in each category can be changed to reflect the requirements of the project phase, the type of change, or tailored to address specific needs/issues of a particular region/department, the categories represent the requirements for successful change and don't change. They provide a consistent framework for evaluating readiness throughout the project.

Readiness Categories Include:

- ❑ Clear Vision and Strong Business Case
- ❑ Leadership Alignment to Support and Drive Change
- ❑ On-Going Change-Specific Communication
- ❑ Stakeholder Engagement
- ❑ To-Be Process and Roles Created and Validated by Business
- ❑ Strong Business Readiness Team(s) and/or Change Networks
- ❑ Organizational Alignment
- ❑ Employee Training & Performance Support

- Clear Program Governance
- Benefits Realization Plan
- Culture of Trust

Readiness Checklist

The table below shows examples of criteria that can be used to evaluate the current state of readiness.

Readiness Requirement	Criteria
Clear Vision and Strong Business Case	❑ Employees can explain the benefits to the organization and to their department
Leadership Alignment to Support and Drive Change	❑ Senior management commitment is visibly demonstrated
	❑ Senior management supports time required for training
	❑ Roles of leaders in supporting a successful implementation are clear and agreed to
	❑ Leadership of each effected group supports the project
On-Going Change-Specific Communication	❑ Clear, concise and timely updates are provided
	❑ People know where to find the information they need
Stakeholder Engagement	❑ Stakeholders are identified
	❑ Stakeholder are involved at appropriate times to build support and readiness
	❑ People are informed about the project and its impact on them
To-Be Process and Role Validation by Business	❑ Processes are defined and documented
	❑ Job Roles are aligned with processes
	❑ Process ownership is clear
	❑ Leaders are willing to reinforce compliance with process

Evaluate Readiness for Launch

Strong Business Readiness Team(s)	❑ A cross-functional team with representation from each effected area has been established
	❑ The role of team members has been defined
	❑ Leadership supports the operations of the team
	❑ The responsibility of each team member in informing and preparing their area for change has been defined
	❑ Team members have received the training required to perform their role
Organizational Alignment	❑ Impact of project on business is understood
	❑ Impact to job roles is understood
	❑ Degree of change required to realize benefits is understood
	❑ New requirement to work in a different way across silos is understood
	❑ Organizational structure required to realize the benefits of the change has been defined
	❑ Changes required in job roles, department operations, policies and procedures have been identified and are supported by management
Employee Training & Performance Support	❑ SOPs and other policy or procedure changes have been made
	❑ Training Plan is finalized
	❑ Training materials are developed
	❑ Reference Guides and/or other Job Aids are available
	❑ Training is scheduled "just-in-time" to prepare people for implementation
	❑ Critical roles that are key to a successful rollout are prepared
	❑ Post go-live Support Plan completed
	❑ Mentors or other resource are available to provide support
	❑ People know who to call for assistance

Program and Governance Team Effectiveness	❑	The process for making decisions is documented and understood
	❑	Decision ownership – and responsibility – is documented
	❑	Criteria and/or other guidelines for making key decisions has been defined
	❑	A process for escalating decisions is in place
	❑	A decision timeline has been established
Culture	❑	Behaviors required to support the change have been identified
	❑	Performance rewards to reinforce new behavior are in place
	❑	People are willing to follow new processes
	❑	People trust that the new system and processes will work
Benefits Realization	❑	A plan is in place to sustain knowledge and ensure that the benefits of the project are realized
	❑	A transition plan for handing responsibility from the project team to operations has been developed

Current Readiness Status Evaluation

Color coding is a good way to create a visual snapshot of readiness. Each category or each check box next to the criteria can be color coded based on the following rating:

■ Not present   ☐ In Progress   ▨ Achieved

Symbols can also be used to indicate the status of each criterion

☒	Achieved
✓	In Progress
❑	Not Started – Not Present

Evaluate Readiness for Launch

The goal is to have all boxes "green" and all criteria achieved before implementation.

Readiness Requirement	Criteria
■ Clear Vision and Strong Business Case	☒ Employees can explain the benefits to the organization and to their department
■ Leadership Alignment to Support and Drive Change	☒ Senior management commitment is visibly demonstrated ☒ Senior management supports time required for training ☒ Leadership of each effected group support the project ☒ Roles of leaders in supporting a successful implementation are clear and agreed to
■ On-Going Change-Specific Communication	☒ Clear, concise and timely updates are provided ☒ People know where to find the information they need
■ Stakeholder Engagement	☒ Stakeholders are identified ☒ Stakeholder are involved at appropriate times to build support and readiness ☒ People are informed about the project and its impact on them
☐ To-Be Process and Role Validation by Business	✓ Processes are defined and documented ✓ Roles are aligned with processes ✓ Process ownership is clear ✓ Leaders are willing to reinforce compliance with process
☐ Strong Business Readiness Team(s)	✓ A cross-functional team with representation from each effected area has been established ✓ The role of team members has been defined ✓ Leadership supports the operations of the team ✓ The responsibility of each team member in informing and preparing their area for change has been defined ✓ Team members have received the training required to perform their role

☐	Organizational Alignment	✓ Impact of project on business is understood ✓ Impact to job roles is understood ✓ Degree of change required to realize benefits is understood ✓ New requirement to work across silos is understood ✓ Organizational structure required to realize the benefits of the change has been defined ✓ Changes required in job roles, department operations, policies and procedures have been identified
■	Employee Training & Performance Support	☐ SOPs and other policy or procedure changes have been made ☐ Training Plan is finalized ☐ Training materials are developed ☐ Reference Guides and/or other Job Aids are available ☐ Training is scheduled "just-in-time" to prepare people for implementation ☐ Critical roles that are key to a successful rollout are prepared ☐ Post go-live Support Plan completed ☐ Mentors or other resource are available to provide support ☐ People know who to call for assistance
☐	Program and Governance Team Effectiveness	✓ The process for making decisions is documented and understood ✓ Decision ownership – and responsibility – is documented ✓ Criteria and/or other guidelines for making key decisions has been defined ✓ A process for escalating decisions is in place ✓ A decision timeline has been established
■	Culture	☐ Behaviors required to support the change have been identified ☐ Performance rewards to reinforce new behavior are in place ☐ People are willing to follow new processes ☐ People trust that the new system and processes will work

▪	Benefits Realization	☐ A plan is in place to sustain knowledge and ensure that the benefits of the project are realized
		☐ A transition plan for handing responsibility from the project team to operations has been developed

Application

As mentioned previously, the Readiness Evaluation is a tool that can be tailored to each department and region affected by the project. It can also be designed to evaluate the readiness level of the entire organization, by defining evaluation criteria that is appropriate for each category.

For example, how will you know that a clear vision and strong business case are understood for your project?

What will leadership do that will tell you they are aligned and supportive of the change?

It's a good idea to compare the readiness criteria you establish with the Critical Success Factors we discussed in Chapter One and with the Impact Analysis we discussed in Chapter Two. This is important because:

   a. The Critical Success Factors describe **what success looks like.**
   b. The Impact Analysis tells you what you **have to be ready for**.
   c. The Readiness Criteria defines what you **have to do to be ready.**
   d. The Readiness Evaluation tells you **if you're on track to being ready** to realize a successful outcome

When these four areas are in alignment, you're on the path to success.

3. WHO DECIDES THAT WE'RE READY?

Although senior leadership is ultimately responsible for making the final go-no-go decision, wise leaders will solicit input from - and listen to - people on the ground who have first- hand knowledge about the current state of readiness.

The Readiness Assessment provides a tool for gathering this information.

Cascading responsibility for evaluating readiness from senior leadership to the department managers to the members of the Change Readiness Team creates a "top down/ bottom-up" decision process and expands ownership for making the right decision.

This approach represents another application of the Organizational Involvement Model discussed in Chapter Four. Everyone has a role in making change work.

The Role of the Change Readiness Team in Assessing Readiness

We've briefly touched on the role of the Change Readiness Team in earlier chapters. We've defined their role as being responsible for informing and preparing employees in their area for changes that will occur, serving as the link between the project team and the employees who will be affected by the project and identifying issues that could prevent a successful implementation.

Many of the readiness requirements listed in the previous section can be met through the work of the Change Readiness Team. They play a major role in identifying issues in their area that could become obstacles to a successful implementation and can be escalated to management for resolution.

Each member of the Change Readiness Team understands, better than anyone on the project team, what is really needed to prepare their area for change. The team is a subset of the larger organization. The attitude and behavior of change team members tends to reflect the attitude of their management toward the project as well as the perceptions of their peers.

> *The Change Readiness Team provides valuable insight into the current thinking of the organization that no one person would have the time to gather on their own.*

Asking each Change Readiness Team member to conduct the Readiness Assessment for their area and then compiling the results from each area

Evaluate Readiness for Launch

into an overall assessment provides an accurate picture of readiness organization-wide.

Cascading responsibility to each manager, to address the areas of low readiness revealed by the assessment, increases ownership of a successful outcome.

Everyone has a role in making change work by ensuring that the requirements for readiness are identified and have been met in their area.

Since change is sustained at the local level, the cascading approach greatly increases the probability of achieving and sustaining the benefits of change in each department company wide.

Cascading Ownership = Success

This was the approach I recommended to the Executive Steering Team and one that they agreed to follow.

Each Executive Steering Team member and senior leader had reinforced their message of the importance of this project to the continued success of the organization, and their expectation of shared responsibility for a successful implementation, by including it as a goal in each department manager's performance evaluation and as a requirement for qualifying for their year-end bonus.

Each department manager was asked to identify an individual from their area to serve as a member of the Change Readiness Team. The importance of this role was reinforced by also including a goal of achieving a successful implementation in each team member's individual's performance plan and linking it to a year-end bonus that people at this level normally did not receive.

This approach turned out to be a critical factor in our success.

We had established a very strong Change Readiness Team with representation from each effected area.

We provided training to prepare them to execute the responsibilities we were asking them to take on.

We developed a Readiness Plan that could be tailored to address the unique cultural differences of each area, prepare for the level of impact they would experience, and meet the readiness requirements for the project.

We had regular meetings where we asked for input on:

1. How things were going overall?
2. What questions or concerns they were hearing from employees in their area?
3. How supportive and engaged their managers were?
4. What could prevent us from achieving a successful implementation in their area?
5. What could we do to address any roadblocks?

In short, each meeting provided us with an opportunity to conduct an informal "readiness evaluation."

We made it a responsibility of the Change Readiness Team to work with their department manager to conduct the formal Readiness Evaluation and develop the Readiness Plan described below for their area.

This plan would be integrated into the overall Organizational Readiness Plan and executed at the local level by the department manager and Change Readiness Team member.

Readiness Plan Outline

The Readiness Plan is basically a template that combines the key steps required to plan for change that we've discussed in previous chapters.

The communication, stakeholder analysis, risks and training sections can be reproduced on Excel spreadsheets making each scalable to accommodate the size of the department or region.

The result is a Readiness Roadmap that provides a consistent framework but allows tailoring to address local differences and different levels of impact.

As mentioned earlier, this is developed by the Change Readiness Team member, reviewed with the management of his/her area, and followed as the plan to prepare for a successful go-live in their department and/or region and to sustain the benefits of the change.

Evaluate Readiness for Launch

Each area's plan can be incorporated into a comprehensive plan to prepare for the rollout enterprise wide, whether a phased, pilot or big-bang approach is used.

Once again, everyone has a role in making change happen

Readiness Roadmap Plan Template

Step 1: Tell the Story: What is changing?

Describe the Change
- What will be different?
  - Process
  - Technology
  - Job Role
  - New Tool
  - Elimination of process, technology, tool etc.
  - Department operations
  - Department structure
  - etc.

Describe the Strategy for implementing the change
- Phased
  - By group?
  - By functionality?
  - Big Bang: Everybody and Everything at the same time?

Step 2: Who is affected? What is the impact? Who can influence the outcome?

List the Stakeholders, Influence and impact
- Those who could affect the outcome (support or impede)

- Those who will be affected by the change *(they will have to do something differently because of the change)*

Example of Stakeholder Analysis

Stakeholder Group (Job role)	Number	Location	Impact from the Change (high, medium, low)	Importance to the Success of the Change (high, medium, low)	Level of Awareness (Aware, Understand Agree, Own)	Level of Support for Change (high, medium, low, none)	Contact

- Who is the Project Sponsor and how is he/she involved in making this project a success?

Step 3: How will employees be informed and prepared?

Describe the Timeline, Process and Key Messages to Communicate with Stakeholders

Example of a Communication Plan

Stakeholder Groups	Announce Objective: Inform	Pre-Go Live: Objective: Prepare	Go-Live	Post Go-Live Objective: Evaluate	Media (Email, meeting, presentation, etc.).	Key Message	Contact
	Date	*Date*	*Date*				

Step 4: What are the Project Risks and Critical Success Factors?

Project/Organizational Risks

What Can Prevent Success?	What Are We Doing to Address this Risk?

Evaluate Readiness for Launch

Critical Success Factors and Measures

How Will we Know We're Successful?	How Will This be Measured?

Step 5: What is the Learning Strategy?

Example of Training Plan

Stakeholder Group	Training Content (key points)	Delivery Method (Group, individual, CBT, Email, etc.)	Delivery Date	Contact

I believe it's beneficial to introduce the template when the Change Readiness Team is established to provide members with a structured overview of the work the team will do.

The timeline for completing the Readiness Roadmap should support the project timeline. It should be reviewed and revised at each project milestone or the completion of each project phase.

4. WHAT DO WE DO IF WE'RE NOT READY?

The Executive Steering Team was pleased with the way the project was going and confident that we would be ready to meet our implementation date.

Our experience with engaging the management level and working with the Change Readiness Team to develop Readiness Plans for each area had gone well.

Management supported the time that was required for their employees to fill this role and saw it as a good opportunity to increase the change readiness skills of their employees and build change capability in the organization that would be beneficial on future projects. Most of the team members saw their participation as a career growth opportunity.

Two members in particular, Rebecca and Carlie, demonstrated exceptional leadership skills and showed the potential to become future leaders of the organization. Even though neither one of them had prior change or project management experience, they learned quickly and could be counted on to meet their deadlines.

I remember my first meeting with the Change Readiness Team when Rebecca spoke up and said "I'm so glad you're here. We need change management because our management really needs to change."

Carlie laughed and said "Rebecca, change management doesn't mean that we actually *change management!*"

She then turned to me with a confused look on her face and asked "Rita, what exactly *does* change management mean?"

After a few weeks of serving on the team, they both understood what change management – and the new term of change readiness that we began using - was all about. They were about to have unexpected opportunities, over and beyond their role on the team, to put their knowledge to work.

We were at the point of doing the final analysis to determine if we were really ready to go live with the project. All signs pointed to go except in two key areas. One area was represented by Carlie and the other by Rebecca. Both of their managers had resigned unexpectedly to start their own company. This left a void in leadership in two high impact areas that you don't want to have when you're about to go live with a project that will change the way a department operates.

An emergency meeting of the Executive Steering Team was called to discuss the possibility of delaying our go-live date until new management was in place.

One option was to continue without leadership in both areas and ask Carlie and Rebecca to assume the responsibilities their managers would have had for implementing the change.

Although this was a lot of responsibility for the two of them to take on, I believed they were capable of pulling it off.

They were respected by their co-workers and had gained credibility from their involvement on the Change Readiness Team. This, combined with the influence of peer pressure we discussed in early chapters, would enable them to successfully pull off more than someone at their level would normally be able to do.

There was a lot of discussion at the Executive Steering Team about Carlie and Rebecca's ability to do this. Most of the executives were in favor of delaying the implementation until new managers could be hired

Evaluate Readiness for Launch

to replace the two who had left unexpectedly. They were concerned that we were setting Carlie and Rebecca up for failure by expecting them to assume so much responsibility.

"We're not ready," Charles, the Senior Leader from the UK stated. "I agree," said Hans, the VP for European Operations. "It's just too risky."

Carlie represented Brussels and Rebecca was in London. Both areas fell into the regions Charles and Hans were responsible for leading. They would have to live with the results of a failed implementation so their opinion mattered.

"Delaying until new managers are hired is not an option," Dennis, the CIO stated. "We have too many other projects in the pipeline that I need to reassign the resources on this project to. Plus, we've already provided training for employees in these areas and if we don't go live soon, they'll forget what they've learned and we'll have to spend more money retraining. We have the momentum we need to continue with this. It's too bad that two key managers have left, but we can't delay."

"Dennis," Charles replied, "this is our region that we're talking about and I think our opinions are the ones that count."

"We've lost two key managers. Rebecca and Carlie are very impressive young women, but we're taking a big risk in entrusting them with this responsibility. I'm not comfortable taking that risk."

"What's our Plan B? " Regina Dion, the VP of Canadian Operations asked. "Surely we have one. "

Everyone looked to Cynthia for an answer.

"We've completed our Readiness Assessment, "she replied, "and the results for Europe are good. Our training sessions were well attended and we have our mentors in place to provide employees with support needed after we go live. Europe appears to be ready, willing and able," she concluded. "I think we should proceed as planned."

"What do you think, Rita, she asked?"

"I believe Carlie and Rebecca can do this," I replied. "We've had very good participation from Europe on our Change Readiness Team. All of the managers have been engaged and are willing to help if needed. I think we've been successful in creating a "change-ready" culture in Europe. Thanks in large part to the work Charles and Hans have done in driving this."

"Charles and Hans," I continued, I understand your concerns. This project will result in a significant amount of change for your areas. We really do need management in place to sustain those changes and it's too bad that we've lost two key managers. However, I believe delaying the implementation until new managers are hired is taking on more risk than we're assuming by trusting in Carlie and Rebecca's abilities to pull this off."

"Also, we've talked a lot about how important trust in leadership is in developing a change-ready organization. We haven't talked as much about how equally important it is that leaders trust their employees. This is a wonderful opportunity to show your trust in Carlie and Rebecca."

"They'll need your support, and this may require more of your time then we had planned, but I believe with your support they will rise to the occasion."

"Why don't we ask them how they feel about doing this?" I concluded.

"I have, "Hans replied. "Neither one expressed any doubts about their ability to do this. They believe they have the support of their co-workers and the other managers. Everyone seems to have rallied around them. Charles and I seem to be the only ones who think we should delay. Although I am concerned, I agree that not moving forward now is taking on more risk than taking a chance with Carlie and Rebecca will be."

The Executive Steering Team made the decision to move forward on schedule as planned. The implementation in Europe went smoothly. Rebecca and Carlie showed exceptional leadership skills. They became super stars and in a few weeks were promoted to the positions their former managers had held.

Trusting in the ability of employees to rise to the occasion is just as important for leaders as trusting leaders to show the way is for employees

Celebrating Success and Moving On

After two previous failed attempts, there was much to celebrate and celebrate we did! Although the work of the project was over, and the members of the project team were moving on to other projects, the work of the organization in sustaining the change so that the benefits of the project could be realized was just beginning.

In the next chapter we'll focus on steps that can be taken to sustain change and create a change ready culture that is a core requirement for surviving and thriving in today's constantly changing workplace.

A Manager's Quick Guide to Achieving Change Readiness

1. Ideally, organizational readiness for change is evaluated as part of the decision to launch a major initiative. Whether or not this is done at the beginning, the evaluation will need to be done before a decision is made to go-live
   a. Is the impact to the organization understood?
   b. Does the organization have the resources required to support this execution of this project?
   c. Does the organization understand what will be required to sustain the benefits once the project goes live?
2. Readiness Criteria is based on the definition of success, and the degree and type of change required to achieve success, and should be evaluated at key project milestones
   a. *The basic categories of readiness typically include vision, stakeholder involvement, leadership support, performance requirements, policy, process and procedure changes, and culture changes*
   b. *Readiness criteria can be tailored to measure the readiness requirements for different regions, functional areas and/or roles, depending on the size and scope of the change.*
   c. *Actions for increasing readiness to the required level for areas that are low should be defined, along with owners who are responsible for each action.*
3. Readiness Criteria, Critical Success Factors and the Impact Analysis should be in alignment.
   a. *The Critical Success Factors describe* **what success looks like.**
   b. *The Impact Analysis tells you what you* **have to be ready for.**
   c. *The Readiness Criteria defines what you* **have to do to be ready.**

d. The Readiness Evaluation tells you **if you're on track to being ready** to realize a successful outcome
4. Readiness is owned by the Change Readiness Team in partnership with their management.
   a. This approach cascades ownership for achieving a successful implementation to the local level where successful change really occurs.
   b. The Change Readiness Team provides valuable insight into the current thinking of the organization that no one person would have the time to gather on their own.

Change Readiness Thinking

Keep the following thoughts in mind to shift your thinking to a Change Readiness Mindset:

1. As people get closer to actually implementing a change initiative, they will come up with all kinds of reasons not to.
2. Being ready to "go-live" with a project means being ready, willing and able to "sustain" the activities that will allow the organization to realize the benefits the project was expected to deliver.
3. Having a Readiness Checklist provides documentation for individuals who are responsible for making the go-no-go decision, and a higher level of confidence that they are making the right decision.
4. Since change is sustained at the local level, the cascading approach greatly increases the probability of achieving and sustaining the benefits of change in each department company wide.
5. It's just as important for leaders to trust their followers as it is for followers to trust their leader.
6. Project Teams that "go-live-and-go-away" have not achieved success. They have only gone live. Accountability for transitioning to people in the organization who will "own" operationalization of the change, and realization of the benefits, should be the responsibility of project leadership.

CHAPTER 7:
SUSTAIN THE CHANGE

"I can't believe we ever did it any other way"

At the end of every project it is beneficial to take a look back at what was learned throughout the implementation process that contributed to a successful outcome and can be repeated on future projects.

It's just as important to have an honest discussion about any problems the project experienced that can be avoided on future projects.

The goal of a Look Back Session is to learn from what didn't work well and not to place blame or find fault with how things were done.

Looking Backward to Look Forward

The information gathered from "look-back" sessions can be leveraged in several ways to help the organization "look forward" at how success can be repeated and change can be sustained. This includes:

1. Reinforcing the behaviors that will support the successful execution of future projects.
2. Producing a project execution guide or standard methodology that employees are expected to follow for all projects.
3. Providing training for employees on how to successfully execute change projects.
4. Sustaining the change readiness knowledge gained by members of the Change Readiness Team by using them as "change mentors" to other projects.
5. Taking all of the steps listed above to build change capability throughout the organization and begin functioning as a change ready organization.

Who Benefits from Lessons Learned?

I don't understand why more organizations don't take advantage of the opportunity to do this at the end of every project, but most don't. The consequence is that any lessons learned remain in the heads of those who learned them - often consultants who take this knowledge with them to benefit other clients.

If the lessons learned aren't documented and don't become institutionalized by the organization, the same mistakes will be repeated by new project teams who don't have access to information from successful projects about how to prepare an organization for change.

Cynthia agreed with my recommendation to conduct a series of "Look Back" sessions after our celebration of a successful launch and before the project team was disbanded and assigned to other projects.

Holding these types of sessions was especially important for Cynthia's project. Since there had been two previous attempts that had failed, senior leadership wanted to understand what we did differently on this project that produced success rather than another failure.

This would also create an opportunity to realize a double benefit from the project. Not only had they been able to achieve a successful execution that would allow them to realize the benefits that had been defined in the shared vision we discussed in Chapter One, they could also leverage this knowledge to reinforce the behaviors that would support the successful execution of future projects and the development of a change ready culture. This, of course, was an extra benefit that hadn't been identified as one of their original goals.

We agreed that participants would include leadership, project team members, change readiness team members and others who had been involved with the project at various times and could provide a different – and possibly more objective - perspective than those who had lived the project day in and day out may have been able to do.

Lessons Learned become Change Readiness Guidelines

The outcome of our look back learning sessions produced the following Change Readiness Guidelines that would be become the expected approach for future projects:

1. Make the vision and benefits of the project crystal clear and relevant to each employee.
2. Assess the impact so an effective change strategy can be tailored that will prepare people for the impact.
3. Ensure top sponsorship and leader alignment throughout the organization by cascading involvement and ownership for readiness in each functional and/or regional area.
4. Establish a Change Readiness Team and Global Change Network consisting of employee representatives to build support and prepare for the transition from the old to the new.
5. Provide timely, clear and relevant communication and plan strategic stakeholder involvement.
6. Deliver sufficient training, preparation and post implementation support through the use of mentors.
7. Establish clear implementation readiness indicators and measurements.
8. Reinforce behaviors required to realize benefits and sustain the change post implementation by aligning performance rewards with the culture changes required to function in the new way.

Sustain the Change

9. Leverage the lessons learned to reinforce the "most effective way" to implement change and institutionalize this approach to sustain success.
10. Develop change readiness capability at all levels of management to create a change ready culture.

Looking Forward

After discussing the results of our Look Back Sessions with the members of the former Executive Steering Team, we all agreed that Guidelines 1 through 7 had been successfully completed. However, the Executive Steering Team members didn't feel as confident that we had achieved success with Guidelines 8, 9 and 10. There was more work to be done before we could say we were "done." This required taking a look forward and what needed to happen over the next few months to sustain our success.

Taking a look back, or conducting what is often called a "Lessons Learned" or "Post-Mortem," is an important step in sustaining knowledge. An equally important step, that is often overlooked, is to take a more formalized approach to looking forward after a project is implemented to evaluate how well the organization has adopted the change.

This can easily be accomplished by establishing future quarterly milestones to evaluate the following

1. Has the desired change become the "new normal" and "just the way things are done around here?"
2. Are you hearing people say "I can't believe we ever did it any other way."
3. Have people slowly reverted to the "old way" or a modification of the "old way" once they realized what living with the new way really meant?

As we said in the previous chapter:

Simply implementing change does not mean that you have been successful. Sustaining that change so that the expected benefits are realized, and it becomes "just the way things are done around here does."

If the answers to questions 1 and 2 above are yes, and the answer to question 3 is no, you're on the right track.

If the answer to question 3 is yes, then you have to ask:

1. What has prevented the change from being sustained?
2. Why has leadership allowed this to happen?
3. What adjustments are required to get back on track to realizing the expected benefits?

Implementing vs. Sustaining

After conducting the Looking Back and Looking Forward exercises on Cynthia's project, it became evident that while we had been successful in implementing the change, more work was required to sustain the change.

We had done a great job of preparing the organization for change. We hadn't put as much focus into identifying or planning for the changes in culture that would be required to sustain the change.

Successfully **implementing** change is an achievement to be celebrated. You'll really know that you've successfully made the change a few months later if you hear people saying "I can't believe we ever did it any other way."

Successfully **sustaining** the change so that it becomes the "new normal," and just the way business is done, requires a change in the culture of the organization.

The next question to be answered by the Executive Steering Team members was: "who is responsible for doing this?"

Who "Owns" Culture Change?

It's rare that a project requiring a technology, process, job role, or some other type of change in operations doesn't also require a change in behavior for the expected benefits to be realized and sustained.

It's also rare that driving the culture change is the responsibility of the implementation team. Their job is to implement. It is the responsibility of the organization, and the leadership of the organization, to create a culture that will sustain the change.

Sustain the Change

This can be planned for in advance by establishing a transition plan from the implementation team to the people in the organization who will be responsible for making the change part of the day-to-day operation of the business.

We had addressed this to a certain extent by establishing the Change Readiness Team and by following our "cascading" approach to extend ownership for a successful implementation to all levels of management.

However, since the focus of the project had not been to change the culture, it would have to become the responsibility of the leadership of the organization to determine how the current culture needed to change to fully realize the benefits of the changes that had now been implemented.

In Chapter Two we talked about how there is no such thing as a "small" change. One change will lead to other changes that will lead to even more changes. The Executive Steering Team was beginning to experience the reality of this statement.

Moving to the "sustain" phase of a project requires more involvement on the part of leadership as the team who was responsible for implementing moves on to the next project.

It was now time for leadership to lead.

An evaluation of the strengths and weaknesses of the current culture to sustain the change and fully realize the benefits of the project was needed. Once we had this information, we could develop a Culture Change Plan to support adoption of the mindset and behaviors that were now needed to sustain success and increase its readiness to benefit from future changes.

Since the work of the implementation team was completed, the Executive Steering Team agreed to form a new team to focus on culture change. This team would consist of members of the Change Readiness Team, representatives from HR and managers of high-impact areas. The Executive Steering Team would continue to exist and would assume responsibility for leading the Culture Change Initiative. Ren Wellington, the Senior Vice President of HR, was asked to join the Executive Steering Team and assume leadership of the Culture Change Initiative. They asked me to stay on and assist them with launching this new initiative. My first challenge was to help them define what we meant by "culture" and how we would go about changing what was once rewarded and required for success, but could now be a roadblock.

Redefining Culture

In its most simplistic terms, organizational culture can be defined as" the way things get done around here." It's the:

- unspoken rules
- sacred cows
- behavior of people who are seen as successful within the organization
- rewards that reinforce what's required to succeed

It's especially important to understand what an organization rewards because this is what reinforces the values, attitudes, beliefs, customs, patterns, ways of doing things, and expectations over time that forms the formal and informal culture of the organization.
This affects:
- how information is shared
- how decisions are made
- how people interact with each other and with stakeholders outside the organization.
- the kind of goals people in the organization pursue
- Ideas about appropriate kinds of behavior to achieve goals.

Since we tend to conform to the behavior of the people around us, culture change is particularly challenging. Everyone is conforming to the current culture which reflects "the way things **were** done around here" and may be what is **still** rewarded but no longer required and, in fact, may even be an impediment to success in the new culture that is required to sustain the benefits of changes in the organization.

Multiple Cultures

Another reason that culture change can be so challenging is that an organization is a conglomerate of many cultures. Each department, region and job role in an organization will have its own unique culture.

Sustain the Change

The way work is done in France is different from the way work is done in Texas. The culture of an Engineering Department is different than that of a Sales and Marketing Department. The culture of Human Resources is very different from the culture of the IT Department.

I've worked with many organizations who wanted to turn their IT professionals into business consultants. They thought that renaming their IT departments Business Solution Groups and calling technology professionals Business Analysts, would accomplish this. This rarely worked because leadership didn't recognize how the culture of the IT department would need to change to support the change in job role. IT professionals weren't prepared to change the thinking and behavior that had once made them successful into the different mindset and behavior that is required for a consultant to be successful.

When an organization is restructured and departments or regions are combined, cultures are also being merged. A new culture will eventually evolve. What type of culture does this need to be to realize the goals of the merger?

When processes are standardized across functions or regions, the change from "my way" to "our way" of working may not be in alignment with the values of the culture of one of the regions or functions who believed that their way was the better way.

When decisions that were once centralized are now decentralized, the culture of the group now having responsibility for making decisions has to change to behave more decisively. When the reverse happens, the mindset of the group losing the power to make decisions has to change so that they don't believe the loss of decision-making authority means that they're less important to the organization.

Changing the culture of an organization is a long term project. Employees need time to get used to the new way of thinking and behaving. For companies with a very strong and specific culture it will be even harder to change.

Organizational leaders must also be cultural leaders and help facilitate the change from the old culture to the new culture. Leadership must model and reinforce the desired behavior, and a critical mass of the organization must be ready, willing and able to adopt the new behavior for culture change to be realized.

Rewarding the New or Reinforcing the Old?

The Executive Steering Team was beginning to see that the old way of thinking and behaving that existed when the project started was not in alignment with how job roles and responsibilities had changed, how decisions will now be made, or how information is being shared now that the project has been implemented.

It was also quite possible that the dysfunction of the old culture may have actually been a driver for the project, but could not be the total solution.

If the same beliefs and behaviors that caused the need for change initially continue to exist, or the project only addressed the "symptoms" of the problem, the project will be seen as a failure.

They could also see that what needed to change now to achieve success were some of the very behaviors that brought success in the past and continued to be rewarded in the present, but would become obstacles to success in the future if a shift didn't occur.

If people who were now responsible for sustaining the change hadn't been involved before go-live, they were more than likely functioning in the old mindset that caused the problems in the first place. They will see no reason to change.

People don't change their thinking, attitudes and behavior overnight.

The requirements and rewards for success had to be redefined to support the behavior required to sustain the benefits of the change.

Evaluating the Culture

The first step we needed to take was to identify behaviors, attitudes and mindset that were required for the change to be sustained but didn't currently exist in the culture.

The next step was to evaluate current performance rewards, eliminate those that don't reinforce the desired behaviors needed and establish new performance rewards that do. This will reinforce priorities and standards throughout the leadership and the workforce.

I designed a ESP Cultural Evaluation that would help them get started.

The table below breaks culture down into different components that may help you assess your current culture and determine how well it supports or prevents the realization of the goals of your project. You can add any terms to each cultural component category that you think are more descriptive of your desired culture. This assessment can be applied to a department, region or to the larger organization

Instructions:

Place an **"E,""S,"** or **"P"** in the box that reflects your current culture. Interpret the results based on the following

- Ideal outcome is a match of **"E's" for "exists"** and **"S's" for "support"**. This element of your current culture doesn't need to change to support the new way of working.
- Place an "**S**" only to describe the culture component you need to create, what needs to be rewarded and what leaders need to reinforce to sustain and/or realize benefits, but doesn't currently exist.
- Place an **"E" and "P"** to indicate that this culture component both "exists" and "prevents" the benefits of the change being realized. This also tells you what you need to stop rewarding. It may have worked in the old world but could be an impediment to sustaining success and realizing the benefits of change in the new world.

CULTURE ESP ANALYSIS

CULTURE COMPONENT 1. Environment	CURRENT STATE E=Exists, S=Supports, P=Prevents
Personal • Like an extended family	
Dynamic and entrepreneurial • People are willing to take risks	

Results Oriented • People are competitive and achievement-oriented	
Controlled and structured • Formal procedures govern what people do	
Other Characteristics of the Environment	

2. Leadership Behavior: How do managers behave in general	**E=Exists, S=Supports, P=Prevents**
Mentoring • Facilitating, or nurturing.	
Entrepreneurial • Innovative, or risk taking.	
No-nonsense • Aggressive, results-oriented focus.	
Coordinating • Organizing, or smooth-running efficiency	
Additional Leadership Characteristics	

3. Management Style is characterized by:	**E=Exists, S=Supports, P=Prevents**
Teamwork • Consensus and participation.	
Individual risk taking • Innovation, freedom, and uniqueness.	
Hard-driving competitiveness • High demands, and achievement	
Security of employment • Conformity, predictability, and stability in relationships.	
Additional Management Characteristics	

4. Organization Glue: Common Values	**E**=Exists, **S**=Supports, **P**=Prevents
Loyalty and mutual trust. • Commitment to this organization runs high	
Innovation and development. • There is an emphasis on being on the cutting edge.	
Achievement • Emphasis on goal accomplishment.	
Formal rules and policies • Maintaining a smooth-running organization is important.	
Additional Values that Hold Us Together	

5. Strategic Emphasis	**E**=Exists, **S**=Supports, **P**=Prevents
Human development. • High trust, openness, and participation.	
Acquiring new resources and creating new challenges. • Trying new things and prospecting for opportunities are valued.	
Competitive actions and achievement. • Hitting stretch targets and winning in the marketplace are dominant.	
Permanence and stability. • Efficiency, control and smooth operations are important.	
Additional Characteristics to Support Growth	

6. Criteria of Success	**E**=Exists, **S**=Supports, **P**=Prevents
Development of human resources • Teamwork, employee commitment, and concern for people.	

Having the most unique or newest products. • It is a product leader and innovator.	
Winning in the marketplace and outpacing the competition. • Competitive market leadership is key.	
Efficiency. • Dependable delivery, smooth scheduling and low-cost production are critical.	
Additional Characteristics that Define Success	
7. Change Readiness	**E=Exists, S=Supports, P=Prevents**
Willing • People want to change	
Able • People have skills and knowledge to change	
Empowered • People feel empowered to change • Supported by Leadership	
Ready • People have tools and resources to change. • The supporting structures and processes are in place and aligned with the change	
Additional Characteristics that Increase Change Readiness	E=Exists, S=Supports, P=Prevents

Redefine Rewards to Redefine Culture

Once you can describe the culture that is needed vs. the one that currently exists, the next step is to develop a plan to begin creating the desired culture. This typically requires redefining rewards to reinforce the new mindset and behaviors that will sustain the change and realize the benefits of your project.

Sustain the Change

As stated earlier, an organization is made up of multiple cultures. It may be that there is only one area where culture change is needed or most critical. It's also possible that the magnitude of the change requires a culture change organization-wide.

The template below may be useful in helping you develop a Culture Change Plan for specific job roles, regions, departments as well as one organization-wide.

It's critical to determine if what you have rewarded in the past will produce the results you need in the future.

CULTURE CHANGE PLAN					
Targeted Area: Region/Role/Department	Current Behavior and/or Mindset	Desired Behavior and/or Mindset	Incentive to Adopt New Behavior and/or Mindset	Reinforcement to Sustain New Behavior and/or Mindset	Metric to Confirm that Desired Behavior and/or Mindset Exists

The Culture Change Initiative was able to conduct the evaluation I designed and identify the cultural changes that were needed and rewards that were required to support the changes in behavior and mindset.

They followed the Change Readiness Guidelines gathered from our Look Back sessions to execute the Culture Change Initiative and gain the support of leadership and engage the organization in looking forward to create this new culture.

Ren Wellington turned out to be an excellent leader who exhibited the characteristics of a "Change Ready Leader" that we will discuss in more depth in the final chapter.

I Can't Believe We Did it Any Other Way!

It's always interesting to check back with clients a few months after a change has been implemented to see if the expected benefits have been realized and sustained or if the change didn't "take" and they've reverted to the old way of doing things.

Of course what I like to hear is that things are going well and they "can't believe they ever did it any other way."

When I checked back with Ren Wellington I found that our project had been successful in delivering the expected benefits from an ROI perspective and also had led to other unanticipated changes – some positive and some not so positive.

Cynthia had been promoted, based on her ability to finally go live with a project that had been unsuccessful on two previous attempts.

The dysfunction of the culture in some areas became much more visible once the project was implemented and the Culture Change Initiative launched. New leadership was required to foster a culture that was much more in alignment with the expanded focus of the company. Turnover in that area had been significant.

> **Even when we are successful in preparing people for change, once the change becomes a reality in their day-to-day world they may realize that it's not how they thought it would be, not the way they want it to be and won't work for them. They no longer "fit" in the new organization.**

After meeting with several of the leaders from our former Executive Steering Team, it was clear that the unanticipated benefit that was realized from the project was an organization that had greatly increased its change readiness capability. They had begun the process of transforming their culture into a change ready culture..

Because of our enterprise-wide engagement strategy and the success of our Change Readiness Network, employees now had a much better understanding of how to prepare for change. In addition to the change readiness skills they developed, they had also been able to combine the tools and approach we used into a repeatable methodology that they had successfully applied to other change initiatives. Having a Change

Readiness Plan for every project had become as common and expected as requiring a budget for every project.

For a culture that had never understood the importance of having change readiness as a core competency, this was quite a change.

What was even more surprising was that Bill, our once most resistant leader to the whole idea of needing to prepare for change, had championed the development of an internal Change Readiness Department and was now the Vice President for Change Readiness enterprise-wide.

I couldn't pass up the opportunity to meet with Bill and hear more about how he was setting up the Change Readiness Department and how he felt about his new role.

"Congratulations Bill," I began, "It's really amazing that you now have a whole department devoted to change readiness. How exciting it must be for you to be in the position of leading the department and seeing the positive impact this will have on the organization."

"It really is Rita," he responded. "I remember when you first came on board and I didn't think anything you said made sense. I thought what you were recommending was totally unnecessary and a waste of time and money. But, after going through the project and seeing what a difference it made to have a Change Readiness Plan and truly understand and prepare people for the impact of change, I became a believer."

"After the Culture Change Initiative was launched and Ren began advocating developing change capability as a core competency for each employee, I volunteered to lead the initiative. The result is this department and my new role," he said proudly.

"I do remember that first meeting and how resistant you were to the idea of focusing on the people issues that could prevent the project from being successful. You've made quite a change yourself," I concluded.

"Yes I have," he responded with a smile. "Now, I can't believe we ever did it any other way!"

Change Brings More Change

It's been said that the only thing that doesn't change is that fact that there will always be change.

This became even more evident to everyone when the company was acquired by another company six months later and a whole new set of post-merger change initiatives were launched.

And so, the cycle of change continued

What had changed for this organization was the ability to be change ready and positioned to benefit from the changes that came their way.

Bill had his work cut out for him – and I was sure he was ready to take on the challenge.

Change Ready Leadership

The organization was able to begin developing a change ready culture because Ren Wellington, as the Senior Vice President for HR, emphasized the development of change readiness as a core competency for every employee in a management position. She was able to marshal the support of executive leadership to launch this initiative because they saw the benefit of becoming a change ready leader themselves.

In the final chapter we'll focus on the skills of a Change Ready Leader and how to become the type of leader that people want to follow.

A Manager's Quick Guide to Achieving Change Readiness

1. The information gathered from "look-back" sessions at the completion of a project can be leveraged in several ways to help the organization "look forward" at how success can be repeated and change can be sustained.

    a. *Lessons Learned become Change Readiness Guidelines for future projects if they are incorporated in to training sessions or used to improve current project management methodologies.*

    b. *It's important to include people outside of the project team who had limited involvement with the project and may be able to provide more objective feedback than someone who lived and breathed the project day in and day out.*

    c. *The consequence of not doing a Look Back Session is that any lessons learned remain in the heads of those who learned them - often consultants who take this knowledge with them to benefit other clients.*

2. We have to look backward to look forward at the steps to take that will increase the level of change readiness in the organization for future projects. The steps are to:

    a. *Make the vision and benefits of the project crystal clear and relevant to each employee.*

    b. *Assess the impact so an effective change strategy can be tailored that will prepare people for the impact.*

    c. *Ensure top sponsorship and leader alignment throughout the organization by cascading involvement and ownership for readiness in each functional and/or regional area.*

    d. *Establish a Change Readiness Team and Global Change Network consisting of employee representatives to build support and prepare for the transition from the old to the new.*

    e. *Provide timely, clear and relevant communication and plan strategic stakeholder involvement.*

    f. *Deliver sufficient training, preparation and post implementation support through the use of mentors.*

    g. Establish clear implementation readiness indicators and measurements.

    h. Reinforce behaviors required to realize benefits and sustain the change post implementation by aligning performance rewards with the culture changes required to function in the new way.

    i. Leverage the lessons learned to reinforce the "most effective way" to implement change and institutionalize this approach to sustain success.

    j. Develop change readiness capability at all levels of management to create a change ready culture.

3. Successfully **implementing** change is an achievement to be celebrated. You'll really know that you've successfully made the change a few months later if you hear people saying "I can't believe we ever did it any other way."

    a. This can be planned for in advance by establishing a transition plan from the implementation team to the people in the organization who will be responsible for making the change part of the day-to-day operation of the business, and just the way business is done.

4. Successfully **sustaining** the change so that it becomes the "new normal," typically requires a change in the culture of the organization.

    a. The requirements and rewards for success may need to be redefined to support the behavior required to sustain the benefits of the change.

    b. It's important to evaluate the performance reward system to determine if you are continuing to reward behavior that brought success in the past but may be an obstacle to sustaining the expected benefits of a project or achieving success in the future.

    c. Changing or redefining the culture of an organization is a long-term project that must be driven and reinforced by leadership to succeed.

Change Readiness Thinking

Keep the following thoughts in mind to shift your thinking to a Change Readiness Mindset:

1. *The goal of a Look Back Session is not to place blame or find fault with how things were done. It is to learn and to leverage what's learned to look forward at how the actions that facilitated success can be repeated on future project.*

2. *Implementing change does not mean that you have been successful. Sustaining that change so that the expected benefits are realized, and it becomes "just the way things are done around here."*

3. *It is often necessary to redefine rewards to redefine culture. Are you reinforcing the old behaviors and mindset or rewarding the new ones that are required for success?*

4. *Even when we are successful in preparing people for change, once the change becomes a reality in their day-to-day world they may realize that it's not how they thought it would be, not the way they want it to be and won't work for them. They no longer "fit" in the new organization and move on to find one where they do – and that's ok.*

CHAPTER 8:
BECOME A CHANGE READY LEADER

"This is a leader I want to follow."

Because successful change begins and ends with leadership, the last chapter of this book could easily have been the first.

The environment that leaders create – through their words – and more importantly through their actions - will support or prevent a change ready culture from emerging.

Employees may or may not listen to what leaders say, but they definitely will pay attention to what leaders do, and will follow their lead.

If leaders aren't change-ready, their employees won't be either. That is why it is critical that leaders model change ready behavior and set an example for employees to follow.

To ensure that change initiatives are successful, organizations must develop a workforce adept at being ready for change in whatever form it takes.

Change agility has to be built into the organization's DNA so they're ready to react quickly as business demands shift. Organizations that are able to respond with agility will be better able to compete in any economy in the global market.

Becoming this type of change-ready, agile company, requires that each organizational level - senior leadership, middle managers and staff - develop change readiness as a core competency. This won't happen without leadership leading the change ready way.

Leaders Leading the Wrong Way

I would like to say that I've seen leadership leading the change ready way in the twenty + years I've been working on large-scale change initiatives. The truth is, I've seen very few. What I have seen too much of are leaders leading the "wrong way."

I describe these leaders as dictators, wimps and un-deciders. They ineffectively attempted to lead change in one or more of the following ways:

1. **Decide and Announce**

    The "dictator" announces that change **will** happen and then assumes his job as leader is done. Typically, nothing is changing in his world so he doesn't understand what all the fuss is about. He sees employees as passive recipients of change who will, of course, follow. It's "his way or the highway." Some do "obey" – out of fear. Most rebel passively and find ways around the change. Others leave because they want to be part of an organization where they have a voice in creating the future. They don't want to be treated like children who are told what to do and expected to obey without questioning. Dictators are a dying breed in today's world where people aren't so willing to trust that what their leaders are saying is the right direction, really is the right direction for them.

2. **Decide and Hide**

    The "wimp" let's people find out through the "grapevine" that change is coming and is never seen or heard from. People feel abandoned and insecure. They begin to make up information about the change because they're not hearing any answers from leadership. "Ring-leaders" emerge to fill the void created by a leader who is in hiding. "We/they" factions develop across the regions, functional areas or even within the department so that there will be someone to blame for change that is doomed to fail due to lack of leadership. Somehow, "wimps" seem to survive. If you're in hiding, you never really threaten anyone. You can come out again when the dust of a failed project settles and the focus shifts to blaming others for an unsuccessful outcome.

3. **Decide and Un-decide**

    The "un-decider" makes a decision and then rethinks that decision and makes another decision. Or, starts a project and then puts it on hold to do more analysis before anything really changes. After a while, people stop paying attention because whatever is decided today will change tomorrow. They become confused about what is and isn't happening, and who is and isn't in charge. The only thing that really changes are the decisions about what to change or how or when to change it. The "un-decider" can survive in cultures where results don't really matter and people want to go through the motions of making change without anything really changing. But, can the organization survive in today's competitive environment with an "undecider" as leader ?

Leaders Leading the Change Ready Way

The leaders I have worked with, who are the kind of leaders people wanted to follow, approached change with a change-ready mindset and behavior that inspired trust and confidence in their followers.

They possessed what I now see as the traits of a Change Ready Leader that can become a model for Change Ready Leadership.

The list below describes what Change Ready Leaders did that less effective leaders failed to do.

1. They were accessible and available to answer questions and provide information that people needed to have something to believe in.
2. They had the ability to see change through the eyes of their employees in addition to viewing it from the perspective of leadership looking across the organization.
3. They could see the big picture as well as understand the challenges that had to be addressed today.
4. They engaged employees in creating the future and treated them as more than passive recipients of change.
5. They were consistent and honest in the message they communicated about the change and its impact on the organization.
6. They modeled the behavior and mindset they needed to have replicated in the organization for the change to be sustained.
7. They trusted their followers.

Creating a Change Ready Culture of Trust and Confidence

The Change Ready Leader's behavior described above created what I consider to be the two most important critical factors of a Change Ready Culture: Trust and Confidence.

> *We often talk about the importance of trusting leadership.*
> *It's just as important that leaders trust their followers.*

How do you build this two-way trust and increase the level of confidence? You build it by sharing information and establishing accountability for a successful outcome throughout the organization.

1. **You show trust in someone by sharing information with them.**

The reason that many leaders fall into the "decide and hide" category described earlier is that they don't have trust or confidence in their employees' ability to deal with the truth about what will change. It's an outdated version of "what they don't know can't hurt them." But, it does.

When information is withheld, people are caught by surprise and are unprepared to handle what comes their way. The leader's belief in their inability to handle change becomes a self-fulfilling prophecy.

When information is shared in an honest, open, consistent and timely manner, people begin to have trust that their leaders know what they're doing and can be depended on to guide them through the ups and downs of change.

This leads to increased confidence that both the leader and employee will be ready, willing and able to handle what comes their way.

2. You increase confidence by holding people accountable for the outcome.

We have a tendency to live up to the expectations others have of us. If someone believes in our ability to be successful, the odds that we will be successful are greatly increased.

A leader shows trust and confidence in their employees' abilities to handle change when they hold them accountable for the outcome. Instead of treating employees as passive recipients of change, as the "decide and announce" leader would do, you're creating shared ownership of the outcome.

When you do this you are also increasing the sense of partnership and creating a culture of "we" that can bridge gaps and build trust across the silos. The belief that "we are all in this together" and have to work together to survive and thrive in a world of constant change is reinforced.

Confidence says that "we are ready, willing and able to handle whatever change comes our way."

When individuals are confident in their ability to handle the unexpected, it's easier to trust others.

Trust and Confidence increase flexibility. When you have a culture of trust and confidence, you will have a culture that is agile and better able to deal with uncertainty and respond quickly and successfully to change

Building Change Readiness into the Organization's DNA

While it's true that change is constant in today's world, it's also true that change is necessary for growth and survival.

Given the rate at which change is becoming "business as usual" in today's competitive and fast paced environment, it becomes increasingly necessary for organizations to build and reinforce change readiness competencies that will facilitate their capacity to accept change as the "new normal."

In addition to leaders setting the example and leading in the "change ready way," change capability must be built into the organization's DNA.

This means that employees at all levels in the organizations must develop change readiness as a core competency. This creates the "culture of we" that is ready, willing and able to make the most of change on a personal and organizational level.

Increasing someone's ability to deal with change in an organizational environment also prepares them to deal with change on a personal level. Thisincreases their confidence in their ability to deal with the unknown and their willingness to trust others.

Although we discussed this briefly in the last chapter on Sustaining Change, it's important to emphasize here that employees may not be able to adapt to change if the design of their jobs doesn't permit it or if they are not given the authority to make the necessary changes to their work needed to achieve the new company direction or focus.

For that reason, organizations need to conduct a high-level overview of jobs considered to be critical to building agility and re-evaluate job descriptions, if necessary.

Finally, organizations have to examine whether their operating model and culture are conducive to change agility and be willing to make the restructuring changes necessary to support the flexibility required for both leaders and employees to be change ready.

Employees should be thought of as future leaders of the organization and taught change ready leadership skills even if they don't currently have the title.

A Culture of "We" Emerges: The Application of Change Ready Leadership

When I heard the news that my client had been acquired by another company I wondered what the impact would be to The Culture Change Initiative that Ren Wellington had launched and if the change ready organization that had began to emerge would survive.

Had Ren really been successful in building change readiness into the DNA of the organization?

I schedule a follow-up meeting with Ren and the former members of our Executive Steering Team to find out.

"Ren," I began, "I know the challenge with post-merger integration is determining how the two organizations will now function as one. "

"Will a "we/they" culture emerge with ongoing battles about how the company will operate, and whose way is the best way, now that the two have become one?"

"Or," I continued, "will the leadership of each organization be able to objectively look at how to take the best of each organization and create one that is stronger and better than either one was individually? What's been your experience here?"

"We had some struggles in the beginning," she responded. "We had launched our Culture Change Initiative and established the Change Readiness Department. We were making real headway into developing change readiness as a core competency for every employee and reinforcing the requirements for our managers and senior leaders to perform as change ready leaders. Then the merger happened and people became more concerned about their own futures and less interested in listening to how we all needed to work together to create an organization we could all feel proud to be a part of."

"That's understandable," I responded. "As head of HR I imagine the responsibility for blending the cultures fell on your shoulders. That must have been difficult," I said sympathetically.

"Not at all," she replied. "I wasn't going to allow that to happen. I wasn't going to take responsibility for an outcome I had no control over."

"Good for you," I responded. "A lot of people in your position would have responded by acting like a victim who had been set up for failure so they could be replaced by someone from the other company. Others would have believed that they could only survive if they seized the opportunity to be a 'star' and not solicit help or involvement from other leaders."

"I did know that all eyes were on me and people were wondering if I would practice what I had been preaching about the qualities of a change ready leader," she continued. "I also knew that if we were to be successful in retaining the best of both cultures, the focus had to shift from 'me' to 'we,' and that had to begin with me and the other senior leaders of both organizations."

"We had to have a shared vision and we all had to have shared ownership of the outcome. I had to have trust and confidence that our leaders and employees would be able to apply what they had learned about the qualities of a change ready leader and survive during the aftermath of the merger."

"How did they do?" I asked.

"Bill was great," she continued. "He rallied the troops around change readiness and established Transition Readiness Teams throughout the organization that included representatives from both organizations. This went a long way in developing the 'we' mentality in the new organization."

"Bill and I also began programs that would teach employees how to apply the organizational change readiness skills they were learning to their personal life. We also worked with the managers on how they could use this expertise to provide support for employees during this time of uncertainty. This made it much more relevant for everyone since none of us were confident we would keep our job."

"Cynthia had challenges with the IT group from the company that acquired us. They didn't see the importance of including change readiness in their project management methodology. With the help of Dennis, our CIO, and Bill, she was able to convince them to 'test' our methodology on the next project. I think this group will take a little longer to get onboard but Cynthia has been a real advocate and is doing a great job in setting an example of a Change Ready Leader," she said proudly.

Thinking back to how resistant Cynthia had been the first day I met her and the challenges we had encountered along the way, I felt proud too.

"What about Charles and Hans in Europe," I asked.

"Well," she responded, "that one has been very interesting. Charles decided to take the package that was offered and the last I heard he was cruising around the world. He said that this was just one too many changes for him to deal with."

"That created an opportunity for the other company to put one of their people in a senior leadership position. They reorganized our operations in Europe and the UK into one organization with Hans reporting to him. It was seen as a demotion for Hans and I was concerned that we would lose him. But, the new guy turned out to be the 'decide and announce dictator' type of leader that didn't work well with our change readiness culture that Hans and Charles had worked so hard to develop in the UK and Europe. He only lasted three months and now Hans is in that position and doing a great job of repairing the 'we/they' relationships that had begun to emerge during the short time the other guy was in charge."

"I remember what a great job Hans did in Europe with our project," I said. "I also remember how Rebecca and Carlie rose to the occasion when their managers resigned and they took leadership for a successful implementation in their departments. We wouldn't have been successful with their help."

"Charles eventually came around with the encouragement of Hans but was never as onboard with our concepts as Hans was. I'm happy that things worked out well for Hans and that Charles made a decision that was probably the best for him and others as well. How are Rebecca and Carlie?," I asked.

"I agree with you about Charles," Ren replied. "He never got in the way of our progress but he never really lead the way either. He was somewhat of a reluctant change ready leader. Fortunately, there was always enough of a critical mass of agreement from the other leaders that he wasn't able to thwart our efforts. Rebecca and Carlie continue to be superstars, in spite of enduring a stressful time while the other guy was in charge."

"Regina has had a challenge with the managers in Canada," she continued. "The company who acquired us had a small operation in Canada and decided to keep Regina as VP of Canadian Operations. The managers from the other company who now report to her have the same dictator style of leadership as the manager in the UK."

"She's asked us to provide coaching and training on Change Ready Leadership to the managers. Bill has been working closely with her as well to develop the change readiness skills of the employees she inherited. Some have embraced the concepts but a few are still resistant."

"She's doing a great job of working with them but is also keeping a close eye on their performance. She's not about to allow anyone to poison the change ready culture she's worked so hard to develop. I'm confident that they will either get on board or we'll help them find another company that values the dictator style of leading change."

"Stan, like Charles, didn't want to go through another big change. He took the severance package that was offered and started his own company. He's kept in touch with Bill and appears to be very successful with his new venture."

"All in all," she concluded, "I think we've done quite well."

"I'm happy to hear that," I replied. "But, I can't help but wondering how things would have turned out if this had happened a year earlier," I asked?

"Oh," she replied empathetically, " I think it would have been a disaster! We didn't have the change ready culture required to be agile enough to deal with all the change that has come about. Our leaders wouldn't have been able to effectively lead their departments during the months of uncertainty, when we didn't know who would stay and who would go, and we would have had much more chaos."

"Because of the work you did with Cynthia's project to introduce the concept of change readiness and the additional work we did to put the structures and processes in place to sustain change, we were able to deal more effectively with this bigger change," she concluded.

"Well, I appreciate the compliment," I replied. "But, you were the one who led the Culture Change Initiative and the company-wide program to develop change ready leaders, change ready employees and, with Bill's help, really build change readiness into the DNA of the organization."

"You're continuing to do that with the employees and leaders of the company who acquired you, which is no small task! Because of your efforts, what will emerge from the merger of the two organizations is a stronger change ready culture that will be better prepared than their competitors to benefit from the opportunities created in our 'new normal' world of constant change," I concluded.

"I hope you're right," she replied. "We still have our challenges with the leadership of the company who acquired us who don't share our values and thinking about how to approach change. Their culture really is a 'decide and announce' type of culture where employees are expected to follow marching orders and not question. This sometimes clashes with the culture of involvement we've worked so hard to develop. I think we're making progress but, quite honestly, there are some days when I wonder if I will survive," she stated sounding a little less confident.

"Ren, I know I'm right. And, I think you will survive. Because what I know for sure, based on what you've accomplished and what you're still accomplishing, is that you **are** the kind of leader people want to follow. That's a skill no one can take away from you, no matter what company you work for, and one that will serve you well whether you stay with this organization or move to one that is better suited to who you are and what you value."

The End is Really the Beginning

As I left Ren's office I thought back to that first cold, rainy day I first started working with this client and how the atmosphere in the meeting room had been just as dreary as the weather outside. The changes that had occurred since that day were remarkable.

It always feels good to complete a successful project. However, the greatest accomplishment is knowing that people have learned change readiness skills through their work on the project that they can apply in both their personal and professional life for the rest of their life.

Real and lasting change happens on an individual level - one person at a time.

Even if Ren, Hans, Bill, Cynthia, Dennis, Rebecca, Carlie and Regina weren't successful in influencing a new way of thinking about change within the new culture that was emerging from the merger, they had been successful in developing an individual change readiness mindset that would give them a competitive advantage in their own career.

They had changed. They were now able to use their change readiness skills to influence others to think about change differently as well.

They are no longer paralyzed by their fear about what's ending, or resistance to what's beginning that could possibly be much better. They have the ability to view change from the perspective of someone who can focus on the opportunities change creates and can therefore benefit.

If things didn't work out for them with the new organization, they have the change readiness skills that would make it possible for them to accept this reality and confidently move on to the next challenge.

Change, after all, is not just an ending. It is also a beginning.

They now knew how to make change work for them. And, in today's world where change *is* the "new normal", that put's you ahead of the game.

Change Ready Individual = Change Ready Leader = Change Ready Organization

I once believed that an individual's level of confidence increased as they moved up the corporate ladder. The higher you climbed the more confident you became.

After years of working with people at all levels, I now realize that there is not a direct correlation between your level of confidence and the level of your position in the organization. Some of the most insecure people I've worked with have held senior management positions in our nation's top Fortune 500 organizations. Confidence doesn't come with the title of leader. And, a leader who lacks confidence will feel too insecure during times of uncertainty to be an effective change leader.

Although it is the responsibility of a leader to inspire confidence in his or her followers, it's difficult to inspire confidence in others if you have little confidence in your own ability to handle change. Being a Change Ready Individual is a pre-requisite to being able to function as a Change Ready Leader.

We look to leaders to make us feel safe and secure. But, leaders are people too with their own fears and insecurities to deal with. If you have the good fortune to work for someone who has the confidence to lead during times of change, consider yourself lucky. You're in the minority. This is becoming rarer in today's insecure workplace of having a job today and being unemployed tomorrow – no matter what your level is in the organization. No one is safe. Job security is a relic of the the past. The reality of today's world is that you can't look to anyone other than yourself to make change work for you. You have to become your own change leader.

Your level of change readiness is in direct proportion to your belief in your ability to deal with uncertainty and emerge on the other side of change stronger and more confident to handle whatever comes your way.

How can you develop this confidence and feel secure during times of change? What can you do if you're working for someone who is shaking in his or her boots and unable to provide you with any support?

Every change readiness principle we've talked about in this book can be applied on an individual level. You can:

1. Create your own vision for the future. If that's taken away from you by the actions of others you can replace it with a new vision. You have the power to create and recreate your future. Remember that change opens the door to opportunities beyond any vision you may have had for yourself.

2. Begin to see the impact of change as the investment required to realize the benefits. You've survived the impact of many changes throughout your life and you will survive many more.

3. Realize that resistance is a normal reaction that will diminish as your realization of potential benefits from change and a new vision of a different future emerges. This will happen when you stop hanging on to something that is quickly becoming the past and not the future.

4. Take ownership of your future by taking ownership of the change. Take the initiative to get involved in what's going on around you. Don't hide. Don't withdraw. Don't surround yourself with people who think the sky is falling and the future is filled with doom and gloom. Don't wait for someone else to tell you what your future is. Get involved in what's going on around you so you can have a voice in deciding what your future is.

5. Equip yourself with the knowledge and skills required to succeed in the new world change creates. Continual learning is required to thrive in today's constantly changing world. Learn as much as you can to increase your value in the workplace of the future.

6. Be ready for change by being prepared. Stay on top of what's going on in your profession and/or industry. Stay connected. The bigger your world of contacts the greater your opportunities. You want to be a person "in the know" and not someone who is caught off guard when change happens.

7. Develop a change ready mindset by changing your attitude toward change. Respond to the unexpected by asking "ok - what's next – what can I do now?" instead of "what's going to happen to me now that I no longer have the future I once thought I had?"

A change ready organization is made up of change ready individuals. Become one and your future will be filled with unlimited possibilities. Before you know it, you will have become the Change Ready Leader people want to follow – whether you have the title of leader or not.

I will leave you with one of my favorite quotes from Helen Keller

"A bend in the road is not the end of the road...Unless you fail to make the turn."

My wish for you is that you will make every change that comes your way a change for the better.

A Manager's Quick Guide to Achieving Change Readiness

1. The environment that leaders create – through their words – and more importantly through their actions - will support or prevent a change ready culture from emerging.
    a. *Employees may or may not listen to what leaders say, but they definitely will pay attention to what leaders do, and will follow their lead.*
    b. *Leaders who lead by behaving like dictators, wimps and un-deciders, are leading change the wrong way.*
2. Change Ready Leaders lead change by:
    a. *Being accessible and available to answer questions and provide information that people need to have something to believe in.*
    b. *Seeing change through the eyes of their employees, in addition to viewing it from the perspective of leadership looking across the organization.*
    c. *Focusing on the big picture as well as understanding the challenges that need to be addressed today.*
    d. *Engaging employees in creating the future and treating them as more than passive recipients of change.*
    e. *Being consistent and honest in the message they communicated about the change and its impact on the organization.*
    f. *Modeling the behavior and mindset they need to have replicated in the organization for the change to be sustained.*
    g. *Trusting their followers.*
3. In addition to leaders leading the "change ready way," change agility has to be built into the organization's DNA so that employees and leaders are ready to react quickly as business demands shift.
    a. *Becoming this type of change-ready, agile company, requires that each organizational level - senior leadership, middle managers and staff - develop change readiness as a core competency.*

b. *Even though they have different responsibilities during times of change, every level of the organization needs to learn change ready leadership skills.*

c. *Organizations have to examine whether their operating model and culture are conducive to change agility and be willing to make the restructuring changes necessary to support the flexibility required for both leaders and employees to be change ready.*

4. Trust and Confidence are critical requirements for a Change Ready Culture

    a. *Trust is built by sharing information.*

    b. *Confidence is increased by holding people accountable for the outcome.*

    c. *Trust and confidence increase flexibility that facilitates change agility and promotes a "we" culture where people work together across the silos to achieve success.*

Change Readiness Thinking

Keep the following thoughts in mind to shift your thinking to a Change Readiness Mindset:

1. *If leaders aren't change-ready, their employees won't be either.*
2. *We often talk about the importance of trusting leadership. However, it's just as important that leaders trust their followers.*
3. *When information is shared in an honest, open, consistent and timely manner, people begin to have trust that their leaders know what they're doing and can be depended on to guide them through the ups and downs of change. This leads to increased confidence that both the leader and employee will be ready, willing and able to handle what comes their way.*
4. *When you have a culture of trust and confidence, you will have a culture that is agile and better able to deal with uncertainty and respond quickly and successfully to change.*
5. *Increasing someone's ability to deal with change in an organizational environment also prepares them to deal with change on a personal level. This increases their confidence in their ability to deal with the unknown and their willingness to trust others.*

HOW TO CONTACT
RITA BURGETT-MARTELL

Rita is a sought-after organizational consultant, coach, thought leader and speaker on strategic change for groups and individuals throughout the world. To learn more about her consulting services or to schedule her to speak at your next meeting, visit her website www.changeguru.com, contact her at rita@changeguru.com or call her at 1-800-441-5981.

Made in the USA
Middletown, DE
31 July 2016